Code Talkers and Warriors

NATIVE AMERICANS AND WORLD WAR II

LANDMARK EVENTS IN NATIVE AMERICAN HISTORY

CROSSROADS SCHOOL

Code Talkers and Warriors

NATIVE AMERICANS AND WORLD WAR II

TOM HOLM

Professor of American Indian Studies
University of Arizona

SERIES EDITOR: PAUL C. ROSIER
Assistant Professor of History
Villanova University

CHELSEA HOUSE
PUBLISHERS
An imprint of Infobase Publishing

In Memory of Kent Ware, Sr.
Kiowa Black Leggings Warrior Society
U.S. Army Air Force, World War II

CODE TALKERS AND WARRIORS: Native Americans and World War II

Chelsea House
An imprint of Infobase Publishing
132 West 31st Street
New York NY 10001

Library of Congress Cataloging-in-Publication Data
Holm, Tom, 1946–
Code talkers and warriors : Native Americans and World War II / Tom Holm.
    p. cm.—(Landmark events in Native American history)
Includes bibliographical references and index.
ISBN-13: 978–0-7910–9340–5 (hbk.)
ISBN-10: 0–7910–9340–9 (hbk.)
1. World War, 1939–1945—Participation, Indian.   2. United States—Armed Forces—Indians.   3. World War, 1939–1945—Cryptography.
4. Indian code talkers.   5. Indians of North America—History—20th century.   I. Title. II. Series.
D810.I5H65 2007
940.54'03—dc22   2006102263

Chelsea House books are available at special discounts when purchased in bulk quantities for businesses, associations, institutions, or sales promotions. Please call our Special Sales Department in New York at (212) 967–8800 or (800) 322–8755.

You can find Chelsea House on the World Wide Web at
http://www.chelseahouse.com

Series design by Erika K. Arroyo
Cover design by Ben Peterson
Illustrations by Sholto Ainslie

Printed in the United States of America
Bang NMSG 10 9 8 7 6 5 4 3 2

This book is printed on acid-free paper.

All links and Web addresses were checked and verified to be correct at the time of publication. Because of the dynamic nature of the Web, some addresses and links may have changed since publication and may no longer be valid.

Contents

Native Americans in the U.S. Armed Forces

Despite the lapse of time and the rise of a more culturally sensitive political environment in the United States, the image of the Native American as a barrier to westward expansion still prevails. In American folklore, Indians have attacked peaceful wagon trains, murdered white children, scalped innocent pioneers, taken hapless would-be Davy Crocketts and Daniel Boones and roasted them at the stake, and treacherously killed thousands of gallant soldiers in unprovoked ambushes. These old and tired images have been a permanent feature of hundreds of books, stage plays, television programs, and motion pictures.

These images are inaccurate in more ways than one: There are very few recorded Indian attacks on wagon trains; Native Americans more often than not adopted white children rather than killed them; the practice of scalping was perpetrated by British colonial, American, Spanish, and Mexican bounties placed on *Indian* scalps; and most frontiersmen married into the tribes as opposed to being tortured by them. Additionally, Native Americans stood with the Americans in all of their wars—even wars against other Native Americans—many more times than they fought against them.

THE COLONIAL PERIOD

The use of Native American warriors as military allies and auxiliaries began long before the American Revolution. Hernán Cortés's conquest of the Aztec Empire in Mexico was as much a result of a smallpox epidemic and of his diplomatic relations with and military aid from Aztec enemies as it was a result of Spanish steel, horses, and gunpowder.[1] When

From the time the first European settlers arrived in the Americas in the late 1400s, they used Native American warriors to help in the conquest of other native groups. For example, a contingent of Narragansett and Mohican warriors accompanied Captain John Mason during the Puritans' attack on a Pequot village on the Mystic River in 1637.

the Puritans massacred the residents of a Pequot village on the Mystic River in 1637, a contingent of Narragansett and Mohican (politically dissident Pequots themselves) warriors accompanied them. It might be added that these warriors were horrified by the Puritans' appalling actions.[2]

During the series of wars that pitted the British against the French in the first 60 years or so of the eighteenth century, both sides used native auxiliaries as scouts, sharpshooters (snipers), and skirmishers—combat activities new to European warfare but long used by Native Americans. At the time, European armies typically employed linear tactics in which armies marched up to each other and slugged it out with muskets at very close range. The forests of North America made traditional European military maneuvers virtually impossible. Consequently, native scouts uncovered enemy positions; native sharpshooters took aim at opposing battlefield commanders; and native skirmishers used cover, concealment, and quiet movement to engage enemy troops, randomly firing from newly acquired guns in order to confuse and frighten them into retreat.[3] It was exactly these tactics employed by native warriors that led to General Edward Braddock's defeat in 1755. Although the British went on to defeat the French in the so-called French and Indian War, they did so only at great cost—in terms of lives and money—and with the help of their own Native American allies.[4] The cost of the war was so great that the taxes imposed on the American colonists to pay for the war became an underlying reason for the American Revolution.

THE AMERICAN REVOLUTION THROUGH THE WAR OF 1812

By the time of the start of the American Revolution in 1775, whites had developed very distinct images of Native American warriors and ideas about warrior tactics. In 1799, Colonel James Smith, who had been an American commander during the war, wrote a narrative of his captivity as a young man by Native Americans, as well as a treatise on warfare using native tactics. In 1755, Smith was a teenage laborer clearing a road for a colonial militia in western Pennsylvania. A contingent of Caughnawaga Mohawk, Mohican, and Delaware warriors captured him immediately before their participation in General Braddock's defeat. The Caughnawagas adopted him and he lived among them as a tribal member for seven years.

Smith's captivity gave him a great deal of insight into the war-making capabilities of Native American peoples. During the American Revolution, he organized an American unit with the intention of training his non-Indian soldiers to use Native American tactics. In fact, he would imply in his 1799 treatise that were it not for these tactics, the Americans would have lost the war. In other words, skirmishing, sharpshooting from concealment, and scouting staved off the British military until the French could send aid and George Washington could organize the U.S. Army as a European-style combat force.

Smith warned that white commanders typically and incorrectly labeled Native Americans as "undisciplined savages" who could not fight a proper battle. His treatise on the "Indian Mode of Warfare" listed the battles in which Native Americans had overcome or equaled European-style armies at little cost to themselves. Their tactics, he wrote, were superior to those of the Europeans simply because Indians worked together and went into battle unencumbered. More mobile and possessing better systems of communication while on the move (hand signals, animal and bird calls, and mirror flashes), native war parties could "perform various necessary maneuvers, either slowly or as fast as they can run." Moreover, "their officers plan, order and conduct matters until they are brought into action, and then each man is to fight as though he was to gain the battle himself." According to Smith:

The business of the private warriors is to be under command, or punctually to obey orders—to learn to march
a-breast in scattered order, so as to be in readiness to sur-
round the enemy, or to prevent being surrounded—to be
good marksmen, and active in the use of arms—to practice
running—to learn to endure hunger or hardships with pa-
tience and fortitude—to tell the truth at all times to their officer, but more especially when sent out to spy the enemy.[5]

When the American Revolution broke out, the Continental Congress realized that most of the native nations
within or bordering the 13 rebellious colonies honored their
treaties with Great Britain. The nations were thus viewed as
domestic enemies. The Congress also realized that bringing
Native Americans over to the colonists' cause was the wis-
est and safest course of action. The Americans needed native allies—or any allies they could get—to win the war. On
Thomas Jefferson's list of King George III's crimes against
the Americans, as listed in the Declaration of Independence, was the use of "merciless Indian savages" in the war
against the colonies. Almost immediately after the Declaration was signed, however, the Continental Congress authorized George Washington to recruit 2,000 Native American
auxiliaries to counter the British alliances with the native
nations.[6] The first American treaty was with the Delawares
of Pennsylvania and New Jersey.

The war caused deep rifts within many native nations.
The great Iroquois (Haudenosaunee) Confederacy split apart
politically and a very large contingent of pro-British Iroquois
was forced to flee to Canada.[7] The Cherokees in the south
also underwent a serious political division. The war (red) half
of the Cherokee government repudiated the civil (white) au-
thorities and established their own towns along the Chickamauga River in Tennessee. This was akin to, for example, what
would happen if the U.S. State Department, the Pentagon,

and the House of Representatives moved from Washington, D.C., and set up a competing U.S. government in Richmond, Virginia. In fact, the Cherokee split was not unlike what happened to the United States in the Civil War.[8, 9, 10]

After the defeat of the British and the subsequent Treaty of Paris, signed in 1783, the Americans became the masters of not only the 13 colonies, but also the entire vast territory west of the Appalachian Mountains to the Mississippi River. The Americans, however, were masters in name only. The British had indeed ceded these lands to the new United States but King George did not order all of his troops to abandon the forts in the region; nor did he formally abrogate Great Britain's treaties with the Native American nations. The Americans, though, felt that as the conquerors they had immediate political authority over the territory as well as the natives, and that they could, without consultation or the negotiation of new treaties, simply assert their political power and allow American settlement on native lands.

The result of American arrogance and lack of control over white settlement was war. By the late 1780s, the entire western American frontier was in flames. Muscogee Creeks, Shawnees, and the Chickamauga Cherokees raided white settlements in the South, while in the North a large confederation of Miami, Peoria, Shawnee, and numerous other tribes defeated two American armies in what is now eastern Indiana. These defeats in 1790 and 1791 led President George Washington to reassess and change U.S. Indian policies. The treaty-making process was reborn. In the end, new "peace and friendship" treaties were negotiated, more Native American lands were ceded to the United States, and several tribes were won over as allies. In 1794, at the Battle of Fallen Timbers, General "Mad Anthony" Wayne finally defeated the native confederacy that had crushed the two American armies three years before. Wayne forced

(continues on page 16)

THE CHEROKEE WAY OF WAR

When Europeans landed on North American shores, they found the customs, laws, and behavior of the native peoples to be completely foreign and, in many cases, utterly incomparable to Western mores, rules, and actions. Perhaps no greater chasm existed between Native Americans and Europeans than the practice of warfare. In the case of making war, Native American and European differences went far beyond weaponry, tactics, and strategic imperatives. The two groups held fundamentally different views in their reasons for making war.

The Cherokees, who fought French, British, and American troops, practiced a traditional form of warfare that had nothing to do with destroying another nation's army, taking over another country's territory, or even imposing their political will on an opposing state. Cherokee warfare had everything to do with the preservation of domestic harmony and prosperity. In order to understand the Cherokee form of warfare, one must look at the roles, gender obligations, and relationships of Cherokee men and women.

Women were always viewed as the heads, providers, and healers of the Cherokee clans. Not only did they give birth to and rear children, they also raised the corn, pumpkins, and beans that sustained Cherokee life. They served in ceremonial capacities, too, leading the dances of several religious rituals having to do with planting, nurturing, harvesting, and the renewal of Cherokee prosperity. In the long and short term, Cherokee women were associated with life, law, and order.

Men, on the other hand, hunted, fished, and provided for the defense of the villages and the fields. As they aged, they became counselors, religious leaders, diplomats, and spokespersons for the village. Older men might carry the title "Beloved Man," and become ceremonial and magisterial leaders. But because men continued to

(continues)

(continued)

hunt, fish, and make war, male roles were nevertheless associated with killing and chaos—the opposite of women.

Cherokee political life was divided into two distinct councils, or "courts"—the White (Peace) and the Red (War). Neither body was legislative. Cherokees relied on established law rather than creating new regulations, so these bodies were basically judicial by nature. The White Court, made up of a principal chief, two sub-priest chiefs, a council of seven elders representing each clan, and the rest of the male population of the village, set the times for the six major ceremonies of the year, handled disputes that had not been settled by the clans or clan mothers, and had the power to give the Red Court permission to carry out war plans. The Red Court was the war organization that took on the responsibilities of carrying out raids and, by way of diplomacy, making peace. The offices that made up the Red Court were a war chief, a war priest, seven "little captains," a crier, and, most importantly, a beloved woman.

The one who carried the title "Beloved Woman" was an elder and one who had experienced battle and who could therefore speak in both the Red and White courts. Typically she was the person who could instigate aggressive war at the behest of female heads of the seven Cherokee clans. Warfare in Cherokee tradition was made to take captives from enemies to replace clan members who had died. Ultimately, Cherokees went into battle to ease the grief of those Cherokee women who had lost loved ones.

In Cherokee society, grief was seen as a distinct, disruptive force. This viewpoint is expressed in the story of the Sun's daughter. Long ago, the Sun, who was the grandmother of all human beings, took a disliking to her grandchildren on Earth. During her journey across the sky vault, she always paused at her daughter's house at midday. That is when the Sun grew the hottest and the humans on Earth looked up at her and made angry faces. The Sun complained to her brother, the Moon, saying that her grandchildren were ugly and had no respect for her. As a consequence, she decided to punish the humans and stay for longer and longer periods of time at her daughter's house in the sky vault. The heat on Earth caused great suffering. The corn withered and the water in the streams dried up.

Against the warnings of the women, the men on Earth decided to take revenge on the Sun. They went to the Little People for help. These powerful people turned four men into different poisonous snakes who were then directed to lie in wait for the Sun and bite her as she emerged from her daughter's house. In the end, though, the Sun's daughter stepped out and the rattlesnake, being the most aggressive of all the poisonous snakes, charged in and bit her. She died on the spot.

The Sun went into mourning. She hid herself away for seven days. Darkness fell and the cold came. The men finally realized that they needed the Sun for warmth, light, and to make the crops grow in the fields. They vowed to return the Sun's daughter from the western Darkening Land, where the spirits of the dead reside.

Again they went to the Little People, who gave them sour wood sticks and a box. The Little People told them to find the Sun's daughter at a dance, hit her with the sticks, put her in the box, and return her to the East. The Little People also warned the men not to open the box under any circumstances until they returned the daughter to the Sun. They carried out their orders to the letter, even as they listened to the daughter cry day after day on the journey home, begging to be let out of the box because she could not breathe. Finally, the men were fearful of killing the daughter once again, and so opened the box. When they did, out flew a Red Bird. At once the humans knew that no one would ever be able to return from the western Darkening Land again. Upon realizing that her daughter was lost to her once again, the Sun went into a deeper mourning. Chaos ensued and people began to die. In

(continues)

(continued)

desperation, the humans danced and sang year after year until she finally smiled again.

The lesson the humans learned was twofold. First, the dead cannot come back; they can only be replaced with the living. Second, grief, particularly for the proscribed period of time, can lead to chaos and ultimately to death for other human beings. Since Cherokee women raised the crops and nurtured the children, the Cherokees could not afford to have widespread or very long periods of grief.

So, when a beloved woman asked the White Court to declare war so that the Red Court could then plan and execute a raid on a traditional enemy, she was asking the men to "dry the tears" of the women. And when the men returned from a raid, they gave their captives to the beloved woman, who, in turn, distributed the captives to those in mourning for loved ones. The grieving women could then adopt or sacrifice them to the spirit of the dead relative, thus ending the mourning and returning the society to its normal ways. Sometimes an adopted captive would inherit all of the names and even war honors of the deceased person he or she had replaced. When non-Indians began to describe this kind of warfare, they eventually decided to use the terminology *mourning* war.

(continued from page 12)

the tribes' individual members into making peace treaties with and land cessions to the United States. Historians have noted that Wayne's success at Fallen Timbers was in large part due to his Choctaw scouts and auxiliaries.[11]

By and large, Native Americans served with the U.S. military as allies in several wars against other Native Americans. During the War of 1812, for example, Andrew Jackson recruited an all-Cherokee regiment against the Muscogee Creek "Red Sticks." The Cherokee warriors were credited as being among the most valuable soldiers at the Battle of Emuckfaw and in the decisive victory over the Creeks at Horseshoe Bend, both in 1814.[12] A contingent of Cherokees also accompanied Jackson to New Orleans and participated in the 1815 defeat of the British attack on the city. As president, however, Jackson betrayed his Cherokee allies in forcing them to move from their homelands in North Carolina, Georgia, and Tennessee to what is now Oklahoma. That betrayal created the hatred for Jackson that still exists among Cherokees today.

Between 1815 and 1861, Native Americans were recruited on an improvised basis against other Native Americans. Nearly every treaty signed between a native tribe and the federal government contained what amounted to a military assistance clause. As a consequence, while the American frontier moved west, so, too, did the escalation of warfare. For centuries tribes had fought each other in raids and had pitched battles with relatively small numbers of casualties. As whites moved westward, they displaced several Native American nations that, in turn, collided with those tribes long established in the western portion of the growing American nation. The Americans exploited already existing native enmities and called upon their allied Native American nations to participate in the frontier war effort. Warfare became particularly deadly and destructive, far more so than the tribes had experienced in the past. By treaty, many Native American nations had become protectorates of the United States and thus ultimately dependent on the federal government to safeguard the boundaries of the lands they still possessed. In a very real sense, Native American warriors were legally bound by treaty to fight for the United States in order to guarantee the integrity of their national boundaries. For the most part, Native Americans fought as allies, raising their own war parties under their own commanders.[13]

THE CIVIL WAR

The Civil War did not change this pattern of Native American participation in U.S. military operations. Once the Confederate States were organized, however, their central government began to seek treaty alliances with a number of different Native American nations. The Confederacy's focus was on Indian Territory (now Oklahoma) for a number of reasons. In addition to the territory's resources—salt, horses, corn, timber—several of the Native American nations there held slaves and were sympathetic to the South's cause. The Union, after all, had forced the Cherokee, Muscogee Creek, Seminole, Choctaw, and Chickasaw nations from their homelands in the East. Moreover, Southerners thought that these people, along with tribes like the Comanche, Osage, Caddo, and Quapaw could supply the Confederacy with a large and ready fighting force.

The so-called Five Civilized Tribes of Indian Territory (now eastern Oklahoma) raised several battalions of infantry and cavalry. The Confederacy used the old formula of employing native allies and auxiliaries under the control of native leaders. A number of Native American officers rose to command large troop formations. Daniel N. and Chilly McIntosh were colonels who led the two Creek regiments, while John Jumper and J. D. Harris, both lieutenant colonels, commanded the Seminole and Chickasaw battalions, respectively. A non-Indian, Brigadier General Douglas H. Cooper, was the overall commander of the Choctaw-Chickasaw regiments. His rise to command was based solely on his longtime career as the U.S. government agent to the Choctaws.[14, 15, 16]

The Cherokees raised two regiments of mounted soldiers and probably had the most troops under the Confederate banner. They also, consequently, had the most commissioned officers. Perhaps the most famous, Stand Watie, was first a regimental colonel and then was promoted to brigadier

During the Civil War, Confederate colonel Chilly McIntosh led the 2nd Regiment of Creek Mounted Volunteers against the Union Army. McIntosh's unit participated in many battles, including Round Mountain and Old Fort Wayne in present-day Oklahoma and Pea Ridge in Arkansas.

general to command all of the Native American troops operating in Indian Territory. He led his Cherokee Braves, as they were called, in the battles of Chustenalah, Wilson's Creek, Pea Ridge, Big Cabin, and several smaller skirmishes. It was said that Watie used old Cherokee war medicine and could make himself appear on one side of the battlefield when he was really on the other. In June 1865, Watie was officially the last Confederate general to surrender his command to Union forces. Equally famous at the time was Watie's "dashing" chief of scouts, Colonel William P. Adair. Later, Adair would become the assistant principal chief of the Cherokee Nation and, during the 1870s, the acknowledged leader of the Cherokee delegates to the U.S. Congress in Washington D.C.[17]

The Union also recruited Native Americans for exactly the same reasons the Confederacy did, but was much less willing to commission them as officers to lead all-Indian regiments or even companies. During the first years of the war, large contingents of Creeks and Cherokees chose to remain loyal to their treaties with the United States and fled to Kansas. A number of Cherokees and a few Creeks joined volunteer formations, such as the 13th Kansas Infantry. A Creek Micco (religious and civil chief and elder) named Opothleyahola led a large group to Kansas and had to fight Confederate troops, in particular Cherokees and Creeks, every step of the way. His followers, including not only Creeks but also Cherokees and Seminoles, made it to Kansas starving and battle-scarred. They would later form the basis of Union Indian "Home Guards" who returned Indian Territory to the United States.

The Cherokee Home Guards, under white officers, were followers of Principal Chief John Ross, who had repudiated the Cherokee treaty with the Confederacy and was forced to live out the war in Washington, D.C. Ross's personal friendship with Abraham Lincoln allowed him to advise the president on the conduct of the war in Indian Territory. The Cherokee Home Guards, called "Pins" because they wore crossed straight pins on their shirts to distinguish them from their Confederate cousins, were the fighting arm of the Keetoowah Society, an association sympathetic to the Union cause and organized to protect both Ross and the Cherokee Constitution. When Ross left for Washington, Stand Watie assumed the office of principal chief of the Cherokee Nation.

Two of the most notable all-Native American Union formations were Company K of the 1st Michigan Sharpshooters and the Tuscarora Company of the 132nd New York State Volunteer Infantry. The 1st Michigan Sharpshooters was organized in the summer of 1863 and served as a guard detail over the Chicago-based prisoner of war camp that interned a very large number of Confederate soldiers. Company K was made up entirely of Ojibwa people of the Great Lakes area. In March 1864, the regiment was transferred to the Army of the Potomac under the command of Ulysses S. Grant. In May of that year, Grant launched his overland campaign that would eventually win the war 11 months later. Company K fought at the battles of the Wilderness, Spotsylvania, Cold Harbor, and took part in the siege of Petersburg. There, they were in the terrible Battle of the Crater, where they lost several of their number. In the old way, those who were mortally wounded in this battle sang their personal songs in anticipation of death.[18]

The 132nd New York was formed in 1862 and stationed near New Bern, North Carolina, after its capture by Union forces. The Tuscarora Company guarded the Union rail center and occupied an area on Batchelder's Creek. In 1864, Confederate general Robert E. Lee authorized a campaign to capture the rail center and its stockpiled provisions. The center of the attack was Batchelder's Creek and fighting there was as intense as any combat yet experienced by Union troops. The Tuscaroras held the line and one of their officers, Cornelius Cusack, was cited for his valor. Cusack, known as War Eagle, was one of the very few Native American commissioned officers in the Union military. He would later command white troops in the West.[19]

Cusack and the Tuscaroras were part of the Iroquois (Haudenosaunee) Nation—the group that would also produce the highest-ranking Native American officer in

Ely S. Parker (Seneca) served as an engineer during the Civil War and eventually attained the rank of brigadier general. At the time of General Robert E. Lee's surrender in April 1865, Parker was serving as adjutant to his lifelong friend General Ulysses S. Grant and wrote the final draft for the terms of surrender.

the Union Army. A Seneca, Ely S. Parker, served on Ulysses S. Grant's personal staff. He was with Grant from Vicksburg in 1863 to Appomattox in 1865. Parker, in fact, wrote out the instrument of Lee's surrender. He was promoted to brigadier general just before the war officially ended in April 1865.[20]

THE INDIAN SCOUTING SERVICE AND THE ALL-INDIAN COMPANIES OF THE 1890s

As has happened after all of the country's major wars, the U.S. Congress cut military spending following the Civil War. It was cut much too soon, however, because the war had disrupted Native American lives almost beyond repair. In the West, white settlers kept up the demand for land, causing a renewed effort to displace the tribes and carve up their lands into homesteads for white farmers. Several industries followed in the wake of the effort made by the United States to occupy the western lands, including railroads, timber, farming, mining, and ranching. Violence erupted, primarily perpetrated by white settlers on Indians. The U.S. Army was called upon to quell the hostilities, only now on a shoestring budget. The western "Indian wars" were just as bloody and horrific as they had been in the East and the U.S. generals soon realized that Native Americans were quite possibly the only people who knew the land well enough to search out and fight the hostile tribes. The U.S. Army pressured Congress to pass a new military appropriation bill in 1866. One article of the act provided for the establishment of the Indian Scouting Service (ISS). Soon a battalion of Pawnee scouts was protecting the men building the Transcontinental Railroad as it wound its way across the Great Plains, and a company of Seminole and black scouts were formed to fight the tribes of western Texas. Poncas, Osages, and Otoes scouted for the U.S. Army on the Southern Plains, and by the late 1870s, Apache scouts were enlisted to fight against their own kinsmen.

The military record of the ISS is without parallel. Between 1872 and 1890, 16 Native American scouts were each awarded the Congressional Medal of Honor for bravery above and beyond the call of duty. The service was not disbanded until 1943. The previous year, the U.S. Army's Special Forces, which would later gain fame in Vietnam, adopted the Indian Scouting Service's crossed-arrow insignia. The last scout to retire from the U.S. Army was Sergeant William Major, an Apache.[21, 22]

In recognition of the military value of Native American troops as scouts, cavalrymen, and sharpshooters, a bill was introduced in Congress in 1891 to provide for the enlistment of 2,000 Indians into the regular armed forces. Although the bill was not passed, Secretary of War Renfield Proctor nevertheless authorized the enlistment of one company of Native Americans for each of the 26 non-Indian regiments of cavalry and infantry serving west of the Mississippi River. The companies would serve under white officers. Proctor, a firm believer that Native Americans should be assimilated into the culture of the United States, saw military service as a step in the integration process.

Several Native American companies were formed and for another four years proved to be successful. In 1895, however, the all-Indian formations were abruptly disbanded and the Indian soldiers mustered out of the U.S. Army. There were several reasons underlying the decision to dissolve those companies. First, Proctor was no longer secretary of war and most of the generals thought that the army was no place for "social experiments." Moreover, several ranking commanders expressed the opinion that serving with Indians would be detrimental to the careers of aspiring younger officers. Ultimately, disbanding the Native American companies came down to a matter of race. John M. Schofield, commanding general of the U.S. Army, decided to weed out a number of white soldiers to make room for the Native American units. General Hugh L. Scott, who had commanded an all-Kiowa troop of the 7th Cavalry, would later complain bitterly about the disbanding of the Indian companies. "The truth was," he wrote, "that the army was angry at Gen. Schofield for mustering out white men." Scott argued that the army should have been expanded rather than shoehorning the native companies into already standing regiments and replacing the white troops, instead of making room for promotion and advancement. Schofield was probably acting under severe budget restraints as well. The United States experienced an economic recession in the early 1890s and military spending reached a new low.[23, 24, 25] Expanding the military service was virtually impossible. Had the Indian companies not been disbanded, they would no doubt have been employed in the Spanish-American War of 1898.

WORLD WAR I

Somehow the idea of integrating Native Americans into the armed forces so that they would gain full U.S. citizenship stuck with Congress even after the "experiment" of the all-Indian units under white officers had failed. The same idea was not applied to African Americans and they continued to serve in segregated military formations. When the United States entered World War I in 1917, members of Congress, Christian reformers, and Bureau of Indian Affairs employees insisted that Native Americans be integrated directly into all-white regiments.

During the war, 17,000 Native Americans enlisted or were drafted into the U.S. armed forces. Under the federal allotment program, which divided reservations into privately held plots of land, a number of Native Americans were made U.S. citizens; most, however, were not. Only those who were citizens were subject to the draft, but still there was a significant number who were illegally drafted. For the most part, though, Native Americans enlisted rather than waited to be drafted. Many signed up at their boarding schools, their teachers and administrators acting as military recruiters. Indian service during World War I became the rhetorical basis for Congress to pass the Indian Soldiers and Sailors Act of 1919 and the Snyder Act of

1924, granting U.S. citizenship to all Indians who had not yet been given citizenship.

Although nearly everyone, except for a large number of Native American leaders, insisted on integrating Indians into white formations during World War I, Native Americans themselves did not simply blend into the all-white regiments. The idea that they had distinct military capabilities in fact led to the creation of special, and often dangerous, duties for Indians based on racial stereotype. In the four centuries of contact between Native Americans and Europeans, a mythology had been built around the notions that Native Americans were particularly adept practitioners of "woodcraft" as well as being fierce warriors. To their white comrades in arms, they were scouts by nature. A newsletter dedicated to the assimilation of Indians into mainstream American society reported that "Indians in the regiments are being used for scouting and patrol duty because of the natural instinct which fits them for this kind of work." Native Americans were regularly sent into the perilous heart of "no man's land" because of a myth. Unfortunately, the myth persisted through the Vietnam War.

The policy of integrating Indians into white units was modified several times and in many ways. General John J. "Blackjack" Pershing, the commander of the American Expeditionary Force (AEF), brought along a contingent of Apache scouts that he used during his foray into Mexico in pursuit of Pancho Villa in 1916. Large numbers of Native Americans served in the 358th Infantry Regiment, dominated the 36th Infantry Division, and made Company E of the 142nd Infantry Regiment effectively an all-Native American formation. Additionally, a contingent of native soldiers was assigned the duty of "code-talking" by which the U.S. Signal Corps used Native American languages to foil German taps on Allied telephone lines. The Choctaw language became an undecipherable code. Ultimately, their experiences in World War I fostered in Native American veterans a sense of pride in their distinctiveness and their communities' major contribution to the war effort.

But after the Native American doughboys returned from the trenches in France, they did not exactly act in accordance with the wishes of U.S. policy-makers. In 1919, Commissioner of Indian Affairs Cato Sells complained when Native American veterans took part in time-honored tribal ceremonies designed either to honor veterans or purify them of the emotional trauma of combat. Native Americans were, in fact, reaffirming their identities as distinct peoples rather than instantly becoming fully assimilated "Americans."[26]

Nearly the same pattern of Native American service would develop during World War II, but with one major difference: Twice as many Native Americans would serve in both the Pacific and European theaters of the war. Many other native people left their reservations to work in war-related industries, and American Indian service would provide the media with grist for the American propaganda mill. The fact of native service would also bring about an unwanted sea change in American Indian policy. World War II probably marked the greatest change in the lives of Native Americans since Columbus mistakenly identified the Americas for the Indies.

"The Indian Enlists!"

NATIVE AMERICANS BEGAN TO ENLIST IN THE U.S. ARMED forces even before the United States formally declared war on the Axis Powers in December 1941. The U.S. Navy was already in a shooting war in the North Atlantic in 1940 and many admirals and generals were engaged in formulating strategy should the United States become embroiled in a war against Japan or Germany, or both. Despite the strategic debates, reviving the draft, and the cautious overhauling of the U.S. armed forces, when Japan did strike against Pearl Harbor in Hawaii on December 7, 1941, the vast majority of Americans were completely surprised and unprepared for war.

WHY DID INDIANS ENLIST?

For the most part, white Americans were equally unprepared for the enthusiasm with which American Indians came in droves to enlist in the armed forces. The country's enemies were busily issuing propaganda statements urging American racial minorities and various ethnic groups to refuse military service whether by enlistment or by the draft. In the 1930s, the German American Bund, a Nazi organization in the United States, welcomed certain Native Americans as members of a pure warrior race and even had the German minister of propaganda, Joseph Goebbels, proclaim that Indians were honorary Aryans, or members of the same racial group as Germans. When the war started, Goebbels also promised that if Germany won, Native American tribes would get back the land stolen from them.[27]

Richard Neuberger, a freelance writer, offered a rejoinder to the propaganda in the widely popular American weekly magazine the *Saturday Evening Post.* According to Neuberger, a Nazi radio broadcast had "predicted an Indian uprising in the United States," should Native Americans be "asked to fight against the Axis." There was, according to Neuberger, a certain degree of elementary logic in Nazi propaganda. In the name of American progress, Native Americans had been slaughtered, dispossessed of their lands, forcibly stripped of many aspects of their tribal cultures, and left the poorest of the nation's poor. "How could the American Indians think of bearing arms for their exploiters?" Radio Berlin was reported to have rhetorically asked. Neuberger's article emphasized the dramatic side of Native American enlistment, stating that in several places men had arrived at the recruiting stations with their own rifles in hand, ready to be shipped off that very instant to battle the Japanese and German armies. Indians, he asserted, were loyal to the United States because they believed that under Nazi rule they would be enslaved or simply slaughtered.[28]

Had the Germans, or the majority of Americans for that matter, kept up with the history of native service in the armed forces, they would have realized that the majority of Native Americans would join the war effort while others would be reluctant for a variety of reasons. Native Americans did indeed swell the ranks of all the services after Japan struck Pearl Harbor. And, in fact, by late 1942, the numbers

By late 1942, the percentage of Native Americans serving in the U.S. armed forces exceeded that of any other group in the United States. During the war, more than 44,000 Native Americans served in the armed forces, including these Navajos on the island of Saipan.

of Native Americans in uniform not only exceeded expectations but, put on a percentage basis, exceeded the participation ratio of all other U.S. citizens. There were two probable reasons underlying this outpouring of Native American support for the war. The first was economic. Native Americans had been hit hard by the Great Depression, and the military at least offered room, board, clothing, and a paycheck. The second had to do with allegiance to the United States. Since the period of signing treaties with whites, Indians had to look to the federal government to ensure their ownership of what lands they had left after the railroads, farmers, ranchers, and mine operators, and the timber, steel, oil, and coal companies had taken what they wanted.

ARMED NEUTRALITY

Almost from the moment Japan invaded China in 1937, and certainly from 1939, when the war began in Europe, President Franklin D. Roosevelt initiated a program of armed neutrality for the United States. He persuaded Congress to institute programs under which the United States would continue to supply and equip Germany's and Japan's enemies, and effectively placed an embargo on war-related materials shipped to Germany and Japan. In addition to that, he extended U.S. naval protection to shipping on its way to Great Britain. In order to strengthen the U.S. Army, he signed the first peacetime conscription act in September 1940. The Selective Training and Service Act of 1940 would lead to the drafting of thousands of Americans, including Native Americans, into all branches of the U.S. armed forces.

THE IDEA OF ALL-INDIAN MILITARY UNITS

Unlike his predecessors, Commissioner of Indian Affairs John Collier rejected the idea of integrating Indians into white regiments and instead advocated separate Native American military units. Jacob Morgan, the chair of the Navajo Nation, supported Collier's ideas as a practical means of adjusting Native Americans to military service. In his mind, communities of native soldiers would see their way through combat as near complete societies. Morgan thought of the situation in Navajo terms. Navajos, for example, would be better off in units with other Navajos simply because they spoke the same language. If that were the case, training would be easier, because the Native language, whatever it may be—Cherokee, Choctaw, Lakota, Shoshone, Comanche, etc.—would be more readily understood. No time or energy would be wasted on translating commands from one language to another.

Others suggested that Native American cultures would work in favor of all-Indian units. John Collier, for example, thought that unity based on culture would give Native American formations a certain *esprit de corps* that would more or less be based on a sense of ethnic pride. Collier also thought that the special status of Native American nations as semisovereign protectorates justified separate and distinctly Indian military units. He hoped, too, that his government agency, the Bureau of Indian Affairs, would have a much greater say in mobilization that would come with separately organized units of the armed forces. In a way, Collier was looking back at the old American militia system of locally organized companies, battalions, and regiments as a method of maintaining group *élan.* Oliver LaFarge, a leading anthropologist and president of the Association on American Indian Affairs, supported Collier's ideas and further proposed that Indians should be trained separately because of their "differences." By that he meant that cultural values, such as long hair, not eating certain foods, or conducting rituals, might be "incompatible" with standard military routine.[29, 30]

Organizing Native American units was also deemed practical based on the long-held stereotype of Indians as being especially warlike, stealthy scouts, and physically capable of enduring the rigors of combat. According to Stanley Vestal, a leading authority on the tribes of the Great Plains, "The Indian, whose wars never ended, was a realistic soldier," who "never gave quarter nor expected it. His warfare was always offensive warfare." Secretary of the Interior Harold Ickes also wrote about the "inherited talents" of Native Americans that made them "uniquely valuable" to the war effort. Native Americans had, Ickes wrote:

Endurance, rhythm, a feeling for timing, co-ordination, sense perception, an uncanny ability to get over any sort of terrain at night, and, better than all else, an enthusiasm for fighting. He takes a rough job and makes a game of it. Rigors of combat hold no terrors for him; severe discipline and hard duties do not deter him.[31]

Native Americans often accepted these myths about themselves and did their utmost to conform to the "scout-warrior" image. During World War II, the draft was based on a lottery system, under which groups were conscripted according to their birthdays. The dates were literally pulled out of bingo machines, and those men whose birthdays were pulled were called to duty. A Blackfeet man, contemptuous of the Selective Service System, commented, "Since when has it been necessary for Blackfeet to draw lots to fight?" Another tribal elder from Cashmere, Washington, sought to bypass the entire induction and enlistment process and form his own all-Indian scouting corps.[32]

NATIVE AMERICAN MILITARY SACRIFICE

Ultimately, the notion of eventually assimilating Native Americans into mainstream American society worked against the creation of all-Indian military formations. Still, Native Americans volunteered or were conscripted in relatively large numbers. By December 1941, more than two-thirds of all eligible Native American men had registered for the draft. Forty percent of all Crow men were in uniform by the end of 1943, as were 2,000 men from the Pine Ridge, Rosebud, and Standing Rock Sioux reservations. One hundred Ojibwas from Lac Court Oreilles—out of a population of 1,700—were in the military by 1943. Not a single Apache from any of the communities in Arizona, New Mexico, and Oklahoma sought deferments. And, although health problems, poverty, and the lack of proficiency in English led to fairly high numbers of military rejections among some Native American nations, the actual percentage turned out to be less than expected, with a one-third denial rate for the entire native population.[33]

According to Commissioner Collier, there were more than 7,500 Native Americans in the U.S. armed forces as of June 1942, less than six months after the Japanese attack on Pearl Harbor. By October, another observer, Elizabeth Sergeant, a writer for the magazine *New Republic,* reported that the number of Native Americans in the military service had swelled to more than 10,000. By 1944, almost 22,000 Native Americans, not counting those who had become officers, were in the military. At war's end, there were 25,000 to 29,000 enrolled Native Americans serving in the U.S. Army, Navy, Marines, and Coast Guard. According to Veterans Administration sources, at least 44,000 self-identified Native Americans served in World War II. "While this seems a relatively small number," wrote Collier, "it represents a larger proportion than any other element of our population." In short, according to Richard Neuberger, Native Americans were fighting the war "in greater proportionate numbers than any other race."[34]

NATIVE AMERICAN WOMEN AND MILITARY SERVICE

Native American women added their numbers to the U.S. armed forces without having to be drafted. Women in the military were all volunteers, and nearly 800 native women served in the U.S. armed forces during World War II. Elva (Tapedo) Wale, a Kiowa from Oklahoma, signed up with the Women's Army Corps and found herself assigned to an Army Air Force unit. Thus she became an "Air WAC." Another WAC volunteer was Bernice (Firstshoot) Bailey from Lodge Pole, Montana. Bailey joined in 1945 and was part of the Army of Occupation in Germany through the famous Berlin Airlift in 1948–49. Minnie Spotted Wolf from Butte, Montana, was the first Native American to enlist in the Marine Corps

Women's Reserve. Spotted Wolf joined in 1943. She commented that Marine Corps boot camp was "hard, but not that hard." An Oglala Lakota from Pine Ridge, South Dakota, Ola Rexroat became one of the now famous WASPs. This group, the Women's Airforce Service Pilots, were trained aviators who, because they were not allowed to fly combat missions, shuttled aircraft from factories to air bases

Nearly 800 Native American women served in the U.S. armed forces during World War II, including these three Marine reservists in Camp Lejeune, North Carolina. Women held a variety of positions, but the majority served in the Women's Army Corps (WAC), the Women Accepted for Volunteer Emergency Service (WAVES), and the Army Nurse Corps.

and ferried military personnel around the country. Rexroat was assigned the duty of towing targets for aerial gunnery students at the air base in Eagle Pass, Texas. Many Native American women became nurses in the U.S. Army and Navy medical corps. Lieutenant Mabel Aungie, another Lakota from the Rosebud Reservation in South Dakota, served as a nurse for the Indian Health Service under the Bureau of Indian Affairs and joined the U.S. Army in 1942.[35, 36]

THE NATIVE NATIONS DECLARE WAR

In addition to signing up for the war on an individual basis, Native American nations began to assert their sovereign status by declaring war independently of the United States. Within months after the bombing of Pearl Harbor, a number of tribes issued formal declarations of war. Other nations, while not exactly issuing declarations, offered tribal council resolutions guaranteeing their full cooperation in the war effort. Within weeks after the U.S. declaration of war, Jemez Pueblo issued a formal war declaration. In June 1942, the Iroquois Confederacy of New York followed suit. In quick succession, the Michigan Chippewa, Oklahoma Osage and Ponca, and South Dakota Sioux nations all formalized a state of war against the Axis Powers of Germany, Italy, and Japan. These quick declarations were timely announcements of Native American support for the United States.[37, 38] But the Navajos had beaten them all to the punch. In June 1940, the Navajo tribal council, acting to ensure that the Navajo people would cooperate with selective service, declared that there was a "threat of foreign invasion" and that "any un-American movement among our people will be resented and dealt with severely." Moreover,

> We resolve that Navajo Indians stand ready as they did in 1918 to aid and defend our government and its institutions against all subversive and armed conflict and pledge our

loyalty to the system which recognized minority rights and a way of life that has placed us among the greatest people of our race.[39]

Some Native American nations even made cultural gestures to the war effort. In Arizona, four nations agreed to stop using the swastika as a design on their crafts. All of them declared that the Nazis were using the symbol of friendship and the continuity of life "backwards."[40] During the first years of the war, various Native American nations adopted and presented war bonnets to their representatives, and made "chiefs" of Franklin D. Roosevelt, General Douglas MacArthur, Wendell Wilkie, and even Joseph Stalin.[41] First Lady Eleanor Roosevelt was given a Native American name and officially adopted by the Penobscot Nation of Maine.[42]

The Native American record of enlistment and draft registration was not perfect. For the most part, draft resistance in Native American communities during World War II was based on traditional cultural values or the assertion of sovereignty. For example, some Zuni and Hopi men refused to accept conscription for religious reasons. In 1940, 14 Hopis applied for conscientious objector status for religious reasons. Pacifism was and is at the heart of Hopi behavior and all adult males in Hopi society have definite religious duties to perform at certain times of the year. Eight of the Hopis received deferments. The other six tried to avoid prosecution under federal law by hiding in the hills. Eventually they were caught and convicted of draft evasion, spending a year in prison.

Zuni objections were nearly the same as those of the Hopis. The Zunis believed in defensive war and a number of them objected to the draft based on the idea that the Americans were bound to take the offensive on the battlefield. Some Zunis used their status as priests to obtain conscientious objector status and concomitant deferments. When the Zunis requested that all male members of their tribe receive conscientious objector status because they all had religious duties or were members of the priesthood, the selective service officers in Washington refused. Consequently, the Zuni government asserted sovereign authority and created special religious offices that were aimed at getting the individual office holders exemptions from the draft. After the Japanese attacked Pearl Harbor, though, a number of Zuni men accepted conscription or enlisted in the armed forces. By 1945, 213 Zuni men were in uniform, which was 10 percent of the draft-eligible population. There were protests launched by the Tohono O'odham in southern Arizona and by the Haudenosaunee of New York, but by war's end both nations had contributed men, women, money, and even land to the war effort.[43]

Native Americans in the Pacific Theater

ON DECEMBER 7, 1941, THE 1ST JAPANESE AIR FLEET dragged the United States into a world at war. For the first time in history, battles that took place on one side of the globe affected battles fought on the other. Millions had already died.

In the mid-nineteenth century, Japan's rulers began a military, industrial, and social revolution. They opened trade, began to raise individuals to positions of leadership based on merit rather than birth, invested in manufacturing, and started a military building program that would emphasize a strong, technologically oriented navy and a quick-striking, highly trained, and fervently loyal army. The main problem that hindered Japan's economic growth was a severe lack of resources, especially oil, high and low grade ores, smelted and finished metals, and coal. In order to gain and hold natural resources earmarked for economic growth, Japan launched a militaristic policy designed to take control of other lands and resources.

Japan's policy of economic and military expansion led to wars with China and Russia and the takeover of Korea and

Manchuria in the early 1900s. Japan entered World War I on the side of the Allies and, although it did no real fighting, it managed to acquire part of Germany's holdings in the Pacific. These islands, mainly the Bismarcks (near present-day New Guinea), would become a foothold by which Japan would establish a defensive island perimeter surrounding its home islands. By 1940, Japan had invaded China and was rapidly consolidating a large Asian empire. The United States had long since established itself as China's chief protector and ally. Along with its policy of "armed neutrality" toward Germany, the United States clamped a tight embargo on goods shipped to Japan, especially scrap metals and refined oil, in an effort to halt Japanese expansion into resource-rich Southeast Asia. In essence, the United States issued an ultimatum to the Japanese: to get out and stay out of China or live without the resources that drove Japanese industry and sustained its military.[44]

Japanese militarists—who were, more or less, the Japanese government—conceived of a way to fight a war with the United States in the Pacific and win a negotiated peace. The idea was to win in the short term with an all-out surprise attack, quickly destroy U.S. and British naval might, and with success, force the United States to back down from its ultimatum. The Japanese military devised a complicated, swift, and devious attack plan even while its ambassadors in Washington, D.C., were continuing negotiations to restore the dwindling supply of scrap iron and oil. On the morning of December 7, 1941, while their ambassadors were typing out a countermeasure to the U.S. ultimatum, the Japanese struck Pearl Harbor.

Within a span of 10 days, Japanese naval and land forces launched assaults on the Philippines, the islands of Wake and Guam, the Dutch East Indies, Hong Kong, the atolls of Tarawa and Makin, and Malaya. Japanese air power not only had leveled the U.S. airstrip and naval facilities of Hawaii, but

On December 7, 1941, the Japanese bombed Pearl Harbor, Hawaii, which brought the United States into World War II. Pictured here is a rescue party searching for crewmembers of the USS *West Virginia*, which ultimately sank after it was hit by a Japanese bomber.

also sunk two British capital ships, *Prince of Wales* and *Repulse.* By the same measure, the attack on Pearl Harbor cost the United States eight battleships: the *Oklahoma, Arizona, California, West Virginia, Nevada, Maryland, Tennessee,* and *Pennsylvania.* However, only the *Arizona* and *Oklahoma* were destroyed; the other battleships were temporarily put out of commission. Due to a timely delivery of airplanes to Midway Island, the three U.S. aircraft carriers assigned to the

Pacific Fleet were not at Pearl Harbor. The British bastion of Singapore fell on February 15, 1942, and a combined fleet of U.S., Australian, Dutch, and British ships were defeated in the Battle of the Java Sea 13 days later.

The Japanese had "run wild" as their foremost naval commander, Admiral Isoroku Yamamoto, had predicted. In the same breath, however, Yamamoto warned that Japan could not sustain its string of victories. He also hoped that a negotiated peace would come quickly because the industrial strength of the United States and its agricultural, mineral, and human resources would eventually drive Japan to defeat.[45, 46]

Although the attack on Pearl Harbor was the significant event that prompted President Roosevelt to ask Congress for a declaration of war, the assault on the Philippines was perhaps the most humiliating and horrific U.S. defeat in the first months of the war. The few U.S. Marines on Wake Island put up a courageous and tactically smart defense in their loss. In contrast, the defense of the Philippines, while courageous, was overcome because of poor planning and the underestimation of Japanese military strength. Instead of a glorious defeat like that of Wake, the Philippines were lost by way of degrading surrender.

THE BATAAN DEATH MARCH

In 1935, General Douglas MacArthur was offered the job of building the Filipino military into an effective fighting force in anticipation of the United States withdrawing from the country that had been acquired following the Spanish-American War of 1898. MacArthur was an old hand in the Philippines and his task of training the Filipino armed forces was actually helped in July 1941, when the United States incorporated Filipino forces into the U.S. Army. Thus, MacArthur was both a Filipino and an American commander.

The Japanese attacked the Philippines from the air on December 8. The U.S. Asiatic Fleet, then operating in and around the Philippines, promptly withdrew and joined the sea force that was soon to be defeated in the Java Sea. MacArthur, fearing that his air power might be sabotaged, had parked his aircraft in the middle of airstrips, and made sure that they were protected by guards. Because of this mistake, most of the aircraft were destroyed in the first Japanese air strikes. The Japanese landing force hit the beaches on December 10, 1941, and marched directly to Manila, the Philippine capital. MacArthur adopted the notion that he could defeat the Japanese by withdrawing to a position with strong interior lines, where he would wait to launch a counterattack. He pulled back what troops and resources he had left to the Bataan Peninsula and to the island of Corregidor in Manila Bay.

Unfortunately, the defensive lines in Bataan were outflanked and beaten and the Japanese simply shelled Corregidor into submission on May 6, 1942. By then, however, President Roosevelt had ordered the U.S. Navy to extract MacArthur and take him to Australia, where the general vowed to return to the Philippines and drive the Japanese out. With MacArthur giving speeches in Australia, it was left to Jonathan M. Wainwright to be the first U.S. general (other than Confederate generals following the Civil War) to give up his command. Wainwright, although awarded the Medal of Honor after his liberation in 1945, actually was certain that he would face a court-martial for signing the surrender terms.[47, 48]

Keats Begay, a Navajo from the Black Mountain area in Arizona, fought against the Japanese during the invasion, and after the surrender, he survived one of the most notorious and terrible ordeals of World War II, the Bataan Death March. Begay had enlisted in the U.S. Army in March 1941 and after completing basic training was assigned to the 200th Coast Artillery. After a few weeks at Fort Bliss, Texas, the 200th was sent to Angel Island in the San Francisco Bay area. Coastal artillery was appropriately named; it had the big guns along with machine-gun units to provide defense against amphibious enemy troops, as well as air assaults. In September of that year, Begay and the 200th were shipped to the Philippines. The unit was stationed near Clark Air Field and set up as an antiaircraft formation, complete with big searchlights that swept the night sky for enemy airplanes.

In the Japanese air attacks of December 8, 1942, Begay and his comrades in arms fought back with machine guns and antiaircraft artillery shells. Unfortunately, most of their ammunition was blown up on the first day of the Japanese invasion. Thereafter, they became foot soldiers rather than artillerymen. On top of everything else, their food rations began to dwindle, and the Japanese had quickly cut off all outside communications and resupply ships. The air attacks kept up until finally the 200th Coast Artillery moved away from Clark Field and onto the Bataan Peninsula. They had lost many men. During the air attacks on December 8, a 12-man squad from Begay's battery was hauling the gun crew's shells when a Japanese bomb struck them. Everything and everyone was blown up and, according to Begay, "there was nothing left."[49]

The Bataan defense went on for nearly four more grueling months. Begay and his comrades filled in as combat soldiers on the front lines for periods of two weeks at a time. When they were relieved of their positions, they could sleep on cots and take showers. As time and the Japanese attacks wore on, however, both food and ammunition began to run low. The Japanese also attacked the men with words. Japanese radio broadcasts told of great Japanese victories and urged the U.S. soldiers to surrender. Begay listened to an English-speaking woman known to the Americans as "Tokyo Rose." In addition to broadcasting the usual instructions to surrender at once, she spoke directly to the Filipinos, who greatly outnumbered the Americans, saying that Japan was not really at war with them but with the United States. In addition to dropping bombs on the Bataan defense force, Japanese aircraft released leaflets in English urging the Americans to surrender. All a soldier had to do was present one of the leaflets to a Japanese soldier and the American would become a prisoner of war and subject to the treatment outlined in the Geneva Accords. These international rules dealt with the treatment of prisoners of war and dictated that a captive must receive the same rations as his or her military captors. The Japanese military handed out rations to its soldiers that just barely provided enough to sustain their bodies in the field. Because of this, even though they would supposedly be treated the same, the American prisoners were to face near starvation.

After the U.S. Army was defeated at the Battle of Bataan in early 1942, those who surrendered to the Japanese were forced to march nearly 80 miles to Camp Cabanatuan in the northern Philippine province of Nueva Ecija. Among the U.S. troops who had to endure the march were 21 Navajos. Pictured here are U.S. and Filipino troops carrying their fallen comrades in makeshift litters during the march.

Begay endured the fighting and the filth from living in the foxholes of the front lines until April 9, 1942. On that day, the commanders of the Bataan defense force attached a white flag to a pole and surrendered to the Japanese. The Filipino and American defenders, including Begay, laid down their arms. Corregidor held out for another excruciating month.

The Bataan prisoners were moved to the Japanese rear area and were forced to live in the open. Their Japanese guards did not tell them what to do other than sit around and wait. Begay and the other Navajos of his regiment (they numbered 21) discussed an attempt to escape, but since they knew neither the territory nor the language, they decided as a group to remain prisoners of war. At minimum they would receive rations and live in prison camps that were supposed to be cleaner than the foxholes they lived in during the fight for Bataan Peninsula. They did not realize at the time just how wrong they were concerning their imprisonment under the Japanese.

One of the essential conventions of Japanese military service was the notion that unswerving loyalty to the emperor meant that no Japanese soldier should surrender to an enemy. As U.S. Marines and soldiers would later discover, the Japanese often preferred death to surrender. This kind of "death before dishonor" principle led to the Japanese soldiers' deep hatred for those who did surrender, and fueled the rampant mistreatment the prisoners suffered under the Japanese.

The Bataan captives were force-marched some 80 miles in three days, first to Camp O'Donnell then to Camp Cabanatuan. The horrors of the march were many. The prisoners had a small ration of rice to sustain them and were not allowed to drink from the wells along the way. According to Begay, Filipino farmers took pity on the prisoners and left food and water by the trail. However, the Japanese guards ordered the men away from these tiny morsels of food and even kicked them over to make sure that no one would eat except those guarding the prisoners. It made very little difference anyway. Several of the men died of food poisoning they happened to pick up from tainted food they found on the trail. Others caught malaria and dysentery. But the worst of the horrors happened if a man failed to follow the orders of the guards or could not keep on the move due to ill health or hunger. He would be bayoneted to death, his body simply left where he died.

Later, Begay was taken aboard a ship and sent to Japan, then to Korea, and finally wound up in Manchuria. The horrifying treatment continued. After three years of captivity, soldiers from the Soviet Union liberated his prison camp. Begay attributed his survival to his own perseverance and to an object he received from a fellow Navajo soldier. During the prolonged battle of the Bataan Peninsula, two Navajos on guard duty found five arrowheads on a beach. When they returned from the front, they gave one of the arrowheads to Begay. In Navajo tradition, an ancient arrowhead carried with it very powerful protective medicine. The spirits of the ancestors who had made the arrowhead were looking out for him, and all five men who kept the arrowheads survived the death march and three years of harsh imprisonment. All returned to the Navajo Reservation.[50]

The Navajos were not the only Native Americans to take part in the defense of the Philippines and to suffer the cruel imprisonment that followed its collapse. Major Caryl L. Picotte, an Omaha tribal member from Nebraska, was an engineering officer for the Philippine Air Force Depot at Nichols Field (approximately 10 miles south of Manila). After the first Japanese air strikes destroyed the base's aircraft, Major Picotte helped organize an Army Air Corps command to fight as riflemen. This new unit filled in the lines on the Bataan Peninsula and fought from January 1 until the surrender on April 9, 1942.

Like Keats Begay, Picotte was part of the death march to Camp O'Donnell and then to Cabanatuan prison. Unlike Begay, though, Picotte stayed at Cabanatuan until the 6th Ranger Battalion liberated the camp on January 30, 1945. Because he was one of the highest-ranking Native Americans, Picotte attempted to keep an accurate account of all of the men under his command, and he talked to numerous other Native Americans while in prison. He later estimated that more than 300 Native Americans fought in the defense of the Philippines.[51]

One of those 300 who did not surrender was Lieutenant Colonel Edward McClish, a Choctaw from Oklahoma. McClish had been part of the National Guard since 1940. In 1941, he was called to active duty and sent to Panay Island to organize the 3rd Battalion of the Philippine Army. He moved his command to Negros Island, where he was stationed when the Japanese invaded. McClish crossed to the island of Mindanao in late December to add the Moro people's "bolo" battalions to his command. He established his command in eastern Mindanao, but when the Japanese reached Mindanao in April 1942, McClish was in a field hospital and so was not with the 3rd Battalion when it surrendered. As soon as he recovered from his injuries, McClish organized a guerrilla force of some 300 Filipino and U.S. soldiers who had escaped captivity. Soon he joined forces with another American colonel who commanded a large guerrilla contingent in western Mindanao. Together they formed the provisional 110th Division and fought the Japanese until U.S. forces finally landed in the Philippines in 1945. All together, McClish's forces fought in more than 350 engagements with the Japanese. He estimated that during the three years of fighting, he lost 150 men compared to the more than 3,000 Japanese the division killed. Additionally, his men supplied the U.S. troops who landed in the Philippines with valuable information concerning enemy movements, bases, and weaponry.[52, 53]

MIDWAY

The string of Japanese sea, air, and land victories—Pearl Harbor, Wake, Guam, the Philippines, and the Java Sea—ended abruptly within a month of the Corregidor garrison's surrender in May 1942. American signals intelligence and a bold raid on Japan were the primary factors in stopping the Japanese advance. First, the Americans decrypted a Japanese message outlining the plan to land imperial troops at Port Moresby on the big island of New Guinea. This maneuver would threaten Australia and interrupt U.S. shipping in the area. Admiral Chester Nimitz, the commander of Pacific naval operations, decided to counter the Japanese operation by sending two aircraft carriers into the Coral Sea to intercept the Japanese force. The ensuing battle was the first in which the engaged fleets were not in sight of each other. As with several sea battles that would follow, in the Coral Sea operation the principal combatants were the aviators flying off the carriers. On May 7, 1942, American dive-bombers sank a Japanese light carrier. The next day, the Japanese struck the two U.S. carriers, damaging the *Yorktown* and sinking the *Lexington.* Although American losses were actually greater than those of the Japanese, the confrontation succeeded in forcing the Japanese to abandon the Port Moresby landings. What was a tactical loss turned out to be a strategic victory for the Americans.

After their early victories, Japanese strategists had two options. First, they could attack westward toward India and with a victory there possibly knock Great Britain out of the Pacific war. The other attack point was toward the east, either to invade the Aleutian Islands off Alaska or perhaps capture Hawaii. The best option was very likely the westward advance with the possibility of linking up with their Nazi allies in the Middle East, providing, of course, that the German Afrika Corps was victorious in North Africa. The Japanese decided on an eastward attack as a result of the Doolittle Raid of April 18, 1942.

James R. Doolittle, a pioneer aviator and Army Air Force colonel, talked his superiors into the idea of flying B-25 medium bombers off aircraft carriers to attack Japan. It was a terribly risky proposition. No one was really sure that the B-25s could even get off the pitching decks of the USS *Hornet,* the carrier designated as the attack vessel. In any case, the *Hornet* made it through the only break in the Japanese island defensive perimeter at Midway and launched Doolittle's B-25s about 600 miles off Japan's coast. The bombers actually did little damage; the raid did, however, frighten the Japanese general staff into making a bad decision. Elaborate plans for the immediate capture of Midway Island were established and a fleet was sent to attack the U.S. base on the island and draw out what was left of the U.S. Asiatic Fleet for a decisive battle. The Japanese had twice as many carriers and the stronger battle fleet. It was thought that a general engagement would completely destroy U.S. naval power in the Pacific. The actual battle began with a Japanese feint to the Aleutians. They captured the island of Attu principally because the Americans were counting on fighting the main battle at Midway.

American intelligence operations intercepted and decoded a message indicating that a Japanese attack was coming. The trouble was that the Americans did not know the exact target; it had only been deciphered as "AF." A Navy officer tried a "cipher trap" to find out if the attack point would be at Midway, as he suspected. Through a secure telegraph message, he ordered the U.S. radio operations officers on Midway to send a message in plain English saying that the island was short on drinking water. Sure enough, U.S. signalmen intercepted a Japanese message saying that "AF" was running short of fresh water. "AF" was Midway after all.

Operating on this bit of knowledge, Admiral Nimitz put his only three carriers—the *Hornet,* the *Enterprise,* and the newly repaired *Yorktown*—in the vicinity of Midway Island, completely ignoring the attack on the Aleutians. The ensuing battle occurred on June 4–5, 1942. Perhaps the most important result of the Battle of Midway was that U.S. forces destroyed Japan's naval air power. The Americans sacrificed practically all of their torpedo planes, several fighter aircraft, and numerous dive-bombers, but managed to sink four Japanese aircraft carriers—*Akagi, Kaga, Soryu,* and *Hiryo.* The U.S. carrier *Yorktown* was hit hard but was able to stay afloat for two more days. On June 6, 1942, after many bomb and torpedo hits, the *Yorktown* heeled over and sank—the last American casualty of the Battle of Midway.[54]

Among those who fought the Japanese at Midway was Brigadier General Clarence Tinker. An Osage from Pawhuska, Oklahoma, Tinker was the highest-ranking Native American officer at the time. He was also the first U.S. general to die during the war. Tinker commanded the entire Army Air Corps stationed on Hawaii and insisted that he could not lead his men into war without knowing what the war was about. In order to gain this knowledge, he led one of several high-level bomber attacks on the Japanese fleet at Midway. While the bombs from Tinker's B-17s and B-26s did no damage to the Japanese carriers, the airplanes' presence drove Japanese admiral Chuichi Nagumo into making hasty judgments and outright mistakes that would cost him the battle. Tinker was killed when his British version of the B-24D (LB 30) bomber crashed while returning to Hawaii. He was posthumously awarded the Distinguished Service Medal. His courage as well as his demonstrated leadership prompted Commissioner of Indian Affairs John Collier to say that Tinker "exemplified the modern Indian soldier."[55]

The loss of the four carriers was devastating to the Japanese. Japan only graduated 90 to 100 qualified aircraft carrier aviators per year. Within the span of two days, it lost the equivalent of at least three graduating classes of experienced combat aviators. It was a loss that Japan could not make up. After Midway, U.S. generals and admirals were more or less free to pursue just about any strategic advance they wished. The Japanese were still dangerous, but their air power, a key factor to their string of victories, was damaged beyond repair.

THE SOUTHERN PACIFIC CAMPAIGN

As the senior military commander in the Pacific, General Douglas MacArthur decided to initiate an offensive that would advance along a string of islands in the southern Pacific back to the Philippines. This South Pacific attack would begin with taking the islands of Guadalcanal and Tulagi in the Solomons. MacArthur would then work his way up through New Guinea and eventually attack the Japanese naval and air stronghold at Rabaul on New Britain. The attack on Guadalcanal was the first American offensive operation of the war. It began on August 7, 1942, and ended in February 1943. During those seven months, the U.S. Marine Corps, Army, and Navy fought in some of the largest engagements of the war, lived through terrible conditions, staved off several tropical diseases, and emerged bloodied but confident in their abilities as professional fighting men.

The 1st Marine Division made the initial attack on Guadalcanal. Not a lot of resistance was encountered at first, and the marines took the Japanese air base with relative ease. After their initial loss, the Japanese made the old military mistake of "reinforcing failure" and kept pouring troops onto the island. The movement of Japanese troop ships and their escorts accounted for the numerous naval engagements. In terms of intensity and longevity, the combat at sea around Guadalcanal almost equaled that of the struggle on land. The 1st Marine Division was eventually replaced and the 2nd

Marine, the Army's 25th "Tropic Lightning," and Ameri-cal divisions entered the fight. Guadalcanal became an epic struggle through jungle and mountainous terrain.[56, 57, 58]

It was on Guadalcanal that the famous Navajo code talk-ers made their combat debut. War correspondent Richard Tregaskis, in his best-selling book *Guadalcanal Diary*, wrote about the Navajos' preparations prior to landing on the is-land. Tregaskis related the story of a medical officer aboard the troop ship the night before the assault. According to Tregaskis, this officer found the Navajos "doing a war dance" in the hold of the troop ship. One of them, with "a towel for a loincloth and a blackened face," was performing a "cancan while another beat a tomtom,"[59] he said. Tregaskis's mock-ing language and the obvious lack of cultural understanding aside, the Navajos probably were ritually preparing them-selves for the dangers ahead. In addition to carrying out their duties as infantry-trained U.S. Marines, the code talkers car-ried around heavy radio equipment on their backs and were constantly called upon to transmit orders, coordinate artil-lery barrages, and report casualties. They fought off Japanese attacks and were exposed to Guadalcanal's surplus of tropical diseases. In doing so, they perfected their code under battle-field conditions. In the Navajo code alphabet, "Guadalcanal" was translated into "Goat-Ute-Ant-Deer-Apple-Lamb-Cat-Axe-Leg." The code played an integral part in the outcome of the battle, with the code talkers truly earning their share of the victory.[60]

General MacArthur's South Pacific strategy was slow-going and bloody. The combat in New Guinea was especially difficult, because it involved several amphibious landings called "hooks" along the coast, tough slogging through the jungle terrain, and climbing up and down steep, craggy moun-tains. The fighting in New Guinea lasted until war's end. In order to set up the New Guinea invasion, numerous Japanese outposts had to be subdued. MacArthur launched "Operation

Approximately 400 Navajos served as code talkers in the Pacific Theater during World War II. The code talkers were instrumental in helping the United States win many battles and campaigns in the Pacific, incuding Bougainville, which was fought from November 1943 to August 1945. Pictured here: (front row) privates Earl Johnny, Kee Etsicitty, John V. Goodluck, and Private First Class David Jordan; (back row) privates Jack C. Morgan, George H. Kirk, Tom H. Jones, and Corporal Henry Bahe Jr.

Cartwheel" in the spring of 1943. As a consequence, both the U.S. Army and the Marines, along with the Navy's 3rd and 5th fleets under the command of William F. Halsey, fought the battles of Kula Gulf, Woodlark Island, the Bismarck Sea, Rendova, Vella Lavella, Bougainville, and Cape Gloucester in the effort to keep MacArthur's flanks secure. MacArthur had decided that these operations would also neutralize the large Japanese base at Rabaul simply by surrounding it with several island air bases. In this way, the large, isolated Japanese garrison there would "wither on the vine." Operation Cartwheel worked with amazing success.[61, 62]

MacArthur returned to the Philippines in October 1944 with the landings in Leyte Gulf. At the same time, the U.S. Navy fought what would become the largest naval battle of the war. The Japanese, in a desperate attempt to stave off their defeat, launched an operation that very nearly extracted a victory from certain defeat. Two battleship forces were to steam through the many islands of the Philippine group. The first was to navigate through the San Bernadino Strait, turn right, steam into Leyte Gulf, and shell the U.S. Army landing craft. The second battleship force was to emerge from Surigao Strait toward the south and take on U.S. admiral Thomas C. Kinkaid's 7th Fleet, which was operating in support of MacArthur's assault force. A third group was made up of the almost useless Japanese carriers—useless because the Japanese had few carrier-trained, experienced pilots left. This force was intended to draw off the U.S. 3rd Fleet that was guarding the San Bernadino Strait. The 3rd Fleet's commander, Admiral William Halsey, took the bait and went after the decoy aircraft carriers.

After having had one giant battleship, the *Musashi,* sunk from under him, Takeo Kurita, the Japanese admiral leading the force in San Bernadino Strait, emerged to find the sea devoid of U.S. ships. As a result, he turned south to attack MacArthur's landing force. Off Samar Island, the Japanese force encountered the U.S. destroyers and small escort carriers supporting MacArthur's Leyte Gulf landings. This tiny force, designated "Taffy Three," was running out of fuel and ammunition for the embarked aircraft. Admiral Kurita ordered an attack on Taffy Three's aircraft carriers. The U.S. carriers retreated while the aircraft and the destroyers attacked the Japanese force. Some of the aviators actually flew toward the

Japanese ships without ammunition or bombs, buzzing the Japanese commanders to distract them from their focus on the carriers and to prevent them from turning into Leyte Gulf to shell the soldiers moving inland. The destroyers did the same, first putting up a smokescreen intended to camouflage the retreating ships. When the Japanese kept moving toward the gulf, the destroyers *Johnston, Hoel,* and *Heermann* charged out of the smoke toward Kurita's flagship, the *Yamato,* the largest battleship ever built. The Americans fired their guns and torpedoes until they either ran out of ammunition or were put out of action.[63, 64]

The captain of the *Johnston,* Commander Ernest E. Evans, was said to be of Cherokee descent, born in Shawnee, Oklahoma. Evans was a graduate of the U.S. Naval Academy in Annapolis, Maryland, and had been skipper of the *Johnston* since its commissioning. Shells from the *Yamato* and other ships in the Japanese fleet had hit the *Johnston* early in the fight, severely damaging the ship's steering system. Captain Evans, who had been badly wounded, went to the stern (back) of the ship to call down steering instructions through an open hatch to the crew that manned the makeshift rudder mechanism. Time after time, he diverted Japanese attention from Taffy Three's carriers, finally ordering: "Prepare to attack the major portion of the Japanese fleet." The *Johnston* took several shells during its final charge and finally stopped dead in the water. The Japanese concentrated their attack on the ship until it rolled over and sank. In the end, Evans, who had been born in landlocked Oklahoma, followed the tough rule of combat at sea and went down with his ship. For his actions, he was posthumously awarded the Medal of Honor.[65, 66] Although he outgunned the Americans and caused severe damage to their ships, Kurita failed to regroup quickly and did not enter Leyte Gulf. The U.S. ships, commanders, aviators, and sailors had put up the fight of their lives. Admiral Kurita retreated back into San Bernadino Strait.

While the main battle off Samar Island was being fought, Admiral Halsey had found Admiral Jisaburo Ozawa's decoy force and sank four aircraft carriers, a cruiser, and two destroyers. Far to the south, several old U.S. battleships, a few of which had been hit badly at Pearl Harbor three years before, took on the second battle fleet that emerged from Surigao Strait in a night engagement. One by one, the Americans picked off the Japanese ships until the fleet's commander signaled retreat.

THE CENTRAL PACIFIC CAMPAIGN

MacArthur's slow progression northward toward the Philippines had suggested another line of advance across the Central Pacific. If the general was drawing the bulk of Japanese troops into the fight for the Solomons and New Guinea, then another U.S. fleet could initiate an "island hopping" offensive toward Guam and Saipan, two large islands in the Marianas group. From there, U.S. bombers could reach the Japanese homeland. President Roosevelt authorized the offensive and the first Central Pacific campaign with an assault on the Gilbert Islands.[67]

The targets of the Central Pacific campaign were the islands of Tarawa, Makin, Kwajalein, Eniwetok, Saipan, Guam, Tinian, and Peleliu. For Americans, the names of these faraway places may be difficult to pronounce, but they will forever be emblazoned on the battle streamers attached to U.S. Army, Navy, and Marine Corps ship and divisional banners. To start the island-hopping campaign, the 2nd Marine Division landed on Tarawa while the U.S. Army's 27th Infantry Division attacked Makin Atoll on November 20, 1943.[68, 69] As the U.S. Marines and Army advanced on their objectives, the Japanese launched fierce and frenzied "banzai" attacks. These all-out charges, usually undertaken during the early morning hours in total darkness, had been part of the Japanese defenses on several other islands since the Guadalcanal campaign. They were desperate attempts to take as many American lives as possible while trying to preserve the "death before dishonor" code of the Japanese military. In reality, they were suicide missions that left the battlefields carpeted with Japanese dead. Hand-to-hand combat also became common in the battles of the Pacific.

Tarawa and Makin were the last amphibious assaults of 1943. The next step in the Central Pacific campaign was to set up the invasion of the Mariana Islands: Saipan, Guam, and Tinian. These islands were especially important in the campaign. First, the promised long-range, high-altitude B-29 bombers that could fly the round-trip from the Marianas to Japan were just about to start rolling out of the Boeing Aircraft plant. If the Mariana Islands were captured, the air war could be taken directly to the Japanese homeland. Second, Saipan had been in Japanese hands for years and was considered part of the Japanese Empire, rather than just a strategic prize.

Admiral Raymond Spruance was placed in command of the U.S. 5th Fleet and ordered to capture both the Marshall and Mariana island groups. On January 31, 1944, U.S. Marine units attacked Kwajalein. A little more than two weeks later, on February 17, they took Eniwetok. The buildup to taking the Marianas was massive. Spruance's fleet and its amphibious army and marine forces were well equipped for the fight. Spruance had at his command more than 500 ships and 127,000 men. The schedule for the landings was set: Saipan on June 15, Guam on July 21, and Tinian on July 24, 1944.

The Japanese were well aware that the Americans were taking aim at the Marianas. Admiral Ozawa, who would later command the decoy fleet at the battle of Leyte Gulf, planned to wait in ambush to attack Spruance as soon as word came that the Americans were in range of his aircraft. The U.S. Marines landed on Saipan as scheduled.

Four days later, on June 19, Admiral Ozawa opened the Battle of the Philippine Sea off Saipan with air strikes on the

5th Fleet. Rear Admiral Joseph James "Jocko" Clark commanded Task Force 58.1 of the 5th Fleet. Clark, the first Native American graduate of the U.S. Naval Academy, was born at Chelsea, Cherokee Nation, in 1893. He became a U.S. citizen at the age of 14, when the lands of the Cherokee Nation were divided into small plots and handed out to each Cherokee Indian in anticipation of Oklahoma statehood. Clark had commanded a carrier—the new *Yorktown*—and after being promoted to rear admiral in 1944, led Carrier Division 13.[70]

Task Force 58.1 was the major element of Admiral Marc A. Mitscher's Task Force 58. Ozawa began the battle with 300 airplanes attacking in several waves. Clark's carriers launched their aircraft and caught the first Japanese air strike 50 miles from Mitscher's flagship. The result was that of the first Japanese wave, only 20 airplanes got through and inflicted minor damage on the U.S. carriers. Mitscher and Clark sent more and more airplanes into the fight with the major objective of sinking the Japanese aircraft carriers. By the end of the first day, Task Force 58's carrier aircraft had shot down 240 Japanese airplanes. Most important, however, Mitscher and Clark's aircraft had sunk two Japanese fleet carriers, the *Shokaku* and the *Taiho,* the latter being Admiral Ozawa's own flagship.

Ozawa attempted to retreat, but Task Force 58 recovered its aircraft and pursued the fractured Japanese fleet. On June 20, U.S. carrier aircraft found Ozawa's damaged ships and attacked. Having lost nearly all of his airplanes the previous day, Ozawa could not put up much of a fight. The American aviators sank another carrier, the *Hiyo,* and severely damaged two others, the *Zuikaku* and the *Chiyoda.* The airmen also crippled the Japanese battleship *Haruna.* The battle, which U.S. sailors called "the Great Marianas Turkey Shoot," broke the Japanese Navy.[71] As a result, the three-pronged Japanese naval attack on Leyte Gulf was actually a suicide mission. At Leyte Gulf, Ozawa could only use what was left of his 1st Mobile Fleet's aircraft carriers as decoys. All together, the 5th

Fleet destroyed more than 400 Japanese airplanes. "Jocko" Clark's command inflicted the major portion of that loss.

The landings on Saipan, Guam, and Tinian were successful, as was the capture of Peleliu in the Palau Islands. Like Tarawa and Kwajalein before them, all were hard-fought battles. The Japanese lost 4,000 men on Tarawa and 8,000 on Kwajalein; the battle of Saipan cost them even more. When the 2nd and 4th Marine and 27th "New York" Infantry

WHERE THEY FOUGHT IN THE PACIFIC

Many Native Americans fought in the Pacific Theater during World War II, including the individuals and code talker units listed on the facing page. In all, more than 44,000 Native Americans (out of a population of less than 350,000) served during World War II.

assaulted Saipan, the Japanese had a garrison of some 29,000 soldiers. Only about 1,000 of them survived. On top of that figure, 22,000 Japanese civilians died, most by jumping off Saipan's cliffs into the sea and rocky outcrops below. On Guam, the Japanese lost more than 10,000 defenders compared to nearly 1,400 U.S. Marines killed in action. When elements of the 2nd and 4th U.S. Marine divisions landed on Tinian, the Japanese garrison numbered some 9,000

1. Keats Begay (Navajo), 200th Coastal Artillery, U.S. Army. Philippines, Bataan Death March, Korea, and Manchuria.
2. Caryl L. Picotte (Omaha), Army Air Force. Philippines, Bataan Death March.
3. Edward McClish (Choctaw), Guerrilla force, Provisional 110th Division. Negros, Panay, and Mindanao Islands, Philippines.
4. Clarence Tinker (Osage), Army Air Force. Battle of Midway Island.
5. Navajo Code Talkers, 1st, 2nd, 3rd, 4th, 5th, and 6th Marine Divisions. Guadalcanal, Bougainville, Tarawa, Makin, Kwajalein, Eniwetok, Saipan, Guam, Tinian, Peleliu, Iwo Jima, and Okinawa.
6. Ernest E. Evans (self-identified Cherokee), U.S. Navy, USS *Johnston*. Medal of Honor action, Leyte Gulf, Philippines.
7. Joseph James "Jocko" Clark (Cherokee), U.S. Navy, various ships and commands. Battle for the Philippine Sea and numerous aircraft carrier battles.
8. Ira Hamilton Hayes (Pima), 1st, 3rd, and 5th Marine Divisions. Guadalcanal, Bougainville, and Iwo Jima.

Note: Numbers correspond to numbers listed on map; participant's tribe in parentheses.

effective combatants. By the time the island was secured on August 1, 5,000 Japanese soldiers had been killed in action. Between September 15 and October 15, 1944, the 3rd Marine and the U.S. Army's 81st "Wildcat" Infantry Division fought one of the most difficult battles of the Pacific on tiny Peleliu in the Palau Island group. The month-long campaign cost the United States more than 1,200 men killed in action. The Japanese defense of Peleliu was reminiscent of their campaign in Guadalcanal. They reinforced a failed defensive position, and in the process they died on Peleliu almost to a man, losing some 12,000 soldiers.[72]

Meanwhile, MacArthur's brilliant tactics and overpowering use of air, sea, and infantry forces won the long-lasting battle for the Philippines with the capture of the capital, Manila, in March 1945. Although a number of Japanese troops fought until June (and some were still hiding in the jungles as late as the 1970s), the Philippine campaign was arduous but very effective in terms of inflicting casualties on the Japanese. The war for the Philippines cost the Japanese at least 192,000 men between October 1944 and March 1945. American losses were comparatively light: 7,933 killed and 32,732 wounded.[73]

These terrible figures bespeak of the nature of the war in the Pacific. The Japanese were willing to die for their emperor and island nation. Pearl Harbor had angered the Americans far beyond what the Japanese had expected, and when U.S. soldiers saw what had happened to their comrades in arms in the Philippine prison camps, they compounded their anger with deep hatred. The next battles in the Pacific war would be even bloodier.

THE FINAL CAMPAIGNS OF THE PACIFIC WAR

After Peleliu, the South and Central Pacific campaigns coalesced into one grand strategy. At the time, it was thought that two more islands needed to be captured. The first one was Iwo Jima in the Bonin Islands. B-29 raids on Japan had already begun from China, as well as from the islands of Guam, Saipan, and Tinian. Iwo Jima had an airfield and was on the route the bombers took to and from their targets in Japan. American intelligence had also picked up on information that the island was going to be a base for the Japanese suicide aircraft, or *kamikaze* ("Divine Wind"). Kamikaze pilots had already attacked some ships in Leyte Gulf. If Iwo Jima was taken, then the Americans would have a ready-made airstrip to land crippled B-29s or to base short-range fighter escorts for the bombing runs. It would also remove the kamikaze threat.

There were two possible targets for the second island campaign. General MacArthur favored Formosa (present-day Taiwan), a large Japanese-held island north of the Philippines, just off the coast of China. On the other hand, Admiral Nimitz and Admiral Ernest King of the U.S. Navy, advocated invading Okinawa, the largest island in the Ryukyu chain. The Ryukyu Islands were part of Japan. Both the U.S. Army and Navy were looking at either Formosa or Okinawa as the main jumping-off point for the final invasion of the Japanese islands. In the end, Okinawa was selected.

First, though, U.S. forces turned to Iwo Jima. The landings took place on February 19, 1945, but the operation against "Japan's unsinkable aircraft carrier," as it was called by top-tier U.S. commanders, had begun days earlier. On the night of February 16, U.S. Navy underwater demolition and Marine reconnaissance teams went to clear the beach defenses and look over the terrain. A Navajo code talker was with the Marine scouting unit. "Some of the boys," he said, "went all the way 'round the island, scouting to decide where the invasion should take place."[74] Of these U.S. Navy and Marine teams, nearly 200 were killed in accidents or by Japanese patrols.[75] The Navajo code talkers' unit lost 12 out of the 50 men initially sent in. Their reward for scouting the beaches was to be put in the third wave rather than the first wave to come ashore on February 19.

From the start, the invasion was a nightmare. Iwo Jima is a volcanic island with black sand beaches. The sand made it difficult to walk, let alone run, as it continuously caved in upon itself with each footstep taken. Also, the Japanese had literally burrowed through the volcanic rock in a series of hidden and fortified tunnels. Even three full days of bombardment by the U.S. Navy's big guns and carrier aircraft had failed to dislodge the Japanese from their positions. The tunnels ensured that the Japanese had a safe haven for hiding their machine gun, artillery, and mortar positions. The U.S. Marines exposed themselves repeatedly, fighting from one Japanese position to the next. The attempt to bring in tanks was not very successful. The heavy artillery simply bogged down in the sand.

Mount Suribachi was the highest and perhaps most fortified place on the island. The 5th Marine Division was given the assignment of taking Suribachi. The U.S. Marines crawled up the mountain, taking on everything from one-man ambushes from hidden "spider-holes" in the sand, to well-concealed machine-gun positions, to large howitzers firing point-blank from behind thick rock outcrops. Finally, on February 23, men of the 28th Marine Regiment reached the top of Suribachi. Their platoon commander, Lieutenant Harold Schirer, had a small flag that he attached to a long piece of pipe. Three members of the platoon raised the flag, but even before they put it up, the platoon commander sent a detachment down Suribachi to get a larger flag. When the new flag was brought to the top, five marines and a navy corpsman performed a second flag raising. By that time, a marine film crew and Associated Press photographer Joe Rosenthal were there to shoot pictures of the moment. Rosenthal's photograph is probably the most famous to come out of World

War II. It won a Pulitzer Prize and served as the model for the U.S. Marine monument in Washington, D.C.[76]

Of the six who raised the flag, the last man in the group with his hand up but not touching the pole was Ira H. Hayes. According to Alison R. Bernstein, author of *American Indians and World War II,* Hayes "emerged as the most famous Indian soldier of the Second World War," eclipsing the notoriety of even Clarence Tinker, Jocko Clark, and Medal of Honor recipients Ernest Childers, Jack Montgomery, and possible Native American Ernest Evans, commander of the courageous but doomed USS *Johnston.*[77]

Hayes, a Pima Indian from Bapchule, Arizona, enlisted in the U.S. Marine Corps in 1942, shortly after the attack on Pearl Harbor. He had been brought up in a very traditional household on the Gila River Reservation and was a member of the Indian Division of the Civilian Conservation Corps prior to signing up with the marines. After boot camp, he was trained as an infantryman and later attended jump school (paratrooper training), one of the few marines to do so. In fact, the "paramarines" were considered elite among the elite. Hayes was shipped to the Pacific and participated in the capture of Vella Lavella and in the grueling Bougainville campaign. After helping with the flag raising on Iwo Jima, Hayes continued the fight. At one point, according to U.S. Navy corpsman John Bradley, who also took part in the flag raising, Hayes refused to take command of his platoon because, "I'd have to tell other men to go and get killed, and I'd rather do it myself." When Rosenthal's photograph was released, it immediately captured the attention of the American public, the Department of War, and, of course, the president. After 36 days of fighting on Iwo Jima, Hayes, along with Bradley and the only other survivor of the flag raising, Rene A. Gagnon, was ordered back to the United States to appear in war-bond rallies.[78, 79]

Ira Hayes (Pima), who is pictured here at age 19 at U.S. Marine Corps Paratroop School in 1943, was one of six men who helped raise the U.S. flag at Mount Suribachi during the Battle of Iwo Jima in March 1945. After the battle, Hayes was ordered back to the United States, where he participated in several war-bond rallies.

Hayes was not the only Native American on Iwo Jima. In addition to several Navajo code talkers, Louis C. Charlo, a Flathead from Montana, made it to the top of Suribachi just a few minutes after the second flag was raised. Several Native Americans were killed and wounded on Iwo Jima. Two Lakotas, Howard Brandon and Clement Crazy Thunder, Cherokee Adam West Driver, Yurok Eugene Lewis, and Navajo Paul Kinlahcheeny were killed. Clifford Chebahtah, a Comanche from Anadarko, Oklahoma, was a U.S. Marine who saw Hayes and the others raise the flag. "I was lying in a foxhole," he said, "when I saw our boys raise the flag on the top of the volcanic mountain of Suribachi, and cold shivers ran down my spine."[80]

Everyone who landed on Iwo Jima paid a terrible price. Those who were not killed or wounded themselves saw their fellow marines die or suffer injuries under the most horrible of circumstances. In all, 6,821 Americans were killed on Iwo Jima and another 20,000 were wounded. On March 24, 1945, the last pocket of 200 Japanese soldiers made a suicide attack on the marines. They died almost to the last man. Only a handful of the 21,000 Japanese defenders of Iwo Jima lived through the maelstrom of the invasion.[81, 82]

The next American attack was on Okinawa. The battle for the island was even more costly than that of Iwo Jima. The Japanese launched a series of kamikaze attacks that took the lives of several thousand sailors and sank 38 ships. The land battle was just as bad. Two U.S. Marine divisions, the 1st and the 6th, and the 10th Army, especially the 7th "Sight Seeing," the 27th "New York," the 77th "Statue of Liberty," and the 96th infantry divisions saw combat on Okinawa. The United States lost more than 12,000 soldiers, sailors, and marines. When the island was finally secured on June 22, 1945, only 7,000 of the 118,000 Japanese soldiers defending Okinawa had survived. About 100,000 Okinawa civilians died as well.[83, 84]

Okinawa was the last amphibious assault of the war. Unfortunately, the battle may not have been necessary. It was known that the Soviet Union was going to declare war on Japan, and the American B-29 raids on Japan, along with the U.S. submarine war on Japanese shipping, were affecting the morale of Japanese civilians. There were practically no oil reserves, basic ores, or even foodstuffs left. The Japanese people themselves were each living on less than 1,000 calories a day on average—far below what is needed to survive. The final blow to Japan, though, was not the invasion of Okinawa, but rather the effects of the two atomic bombs dropped on Hiroshima and Nagasaki. Japanese emperor Hirohito announced the surrender of the Japanese state on August 15, 1945. The terrible war in the Pacific was over.

The Navajo
Code Talkers

FOR THE U.S. MARINE CORPS, THE WAR IN THE PACIFIC was a great test of its doctrine of amphibious warfare. The U.S. Marines had been under close scrutiny by the federal government, which for several years had been considering the idea of dissolving the branch of service. Originally, the "sea-going soldiers" were placed on ships to provide small arms support to naval cannoneers, boarding parties, and to help keep sailors at their battle stations during ship-to-ship combat. Marines also stood "fire watch" (a duty that continues to this day) to guard against perhaps the most dangerous thing that could happen to a wooden ship. Fire not only would burn a vessel to the waterline, but also touch off its magazine or gunpowder stores and cause an explosion.

AMPHIBIOUS WARFARE

By the early 1900s, some prominent military officials thought that the U.S. Marines had outlived their special position and usefulness. By this time ships were made out of steel and iron and naval doctrine had begun to emphasize the "all-big-gun" battleship, which rendered the small arms, short-range gun-fire of the marines ineffective. The Marine Corps was a small formation limited to duty aboard ships, providing the U.S. Navy with an effective police and prison security force. The only other possible use for marines, it was thought, was to provide small landing forces that could secure beachheads for further army operations. It was in this relatively minor role that the Marine Corps would excel and, luckily for the service, Major Earl Ellis introduced what would become the amphibious warfare doctrine. Ultimately, Ellis's ideas and theoretical understanding of oceanic warfare saved the Marine Corps.

Despite having oceangoing naval vessels for thousands of years, fighting very large battles at sea and maintaining fighting forces that relied on sea power, the nations of the world never really understood the nature of amphibious warfare. The common idea was simply to put a military force ashore and then, once a fortified or entrenched landing area was established, keep reinforcing it until it was strong enough to launch an offensive into enemy-held ground. This method of amphibious warfare resulted in the British disaster in the Gallipoli campaign during World War I. In 1921, Major Ellis presented his marine and naval commanders with the notion that amphibious landings should be tactical maneuvers made from the sea to designated points inland. The water and the beach were places to be crossed using specially designed vessels, vehicles, and weaponry.

The idea was not only novel, but also so obviously practical that the Marine Corps quickly adopted the doctrine as its own. Thus the Marine Corps literally created a place for itself that would enable it to play a significant role in World War II. Basically, marines would move from their vessels behind heavy concentrations of artillery fire (shipboard guns of up to 16-inch caliber) and aerial bombardment to the shore. The marines would be on special landing craft that would allow them to "hit the beach" at a dead run, attacking on a very narrow front. The first group of attackers would be the spearheads driving as far inland as possible. The next "waves" of the attack would be the follow-up troops who would push the main attack forward and provide security on the flanks of the spearhead. In fact, as Major Ellis had anticipated, the only way to defend against this type of attack would be to counterattack on one flank or another in order to cut off the spearhead. Waves of attackers were absolutely necessary for an amphibious assault to be successful.[85]

Essential to amphibious operations were secure, synchronized, and instantaneous communications to coordinate all of the elements of an attack. Shots from the big guns aboard battleships had to be coordinated with air strikes from aircraft carriers and also with the movement of troops from their ships to their assault craft to their landing zones to their inland objectives. Valuable time had to be used in deciphering codes, Morse code blinkers from the ships could easily be read, and English transmissions could be translated by the Japanese in real time.

THE SELECTION OF NAVAJO AS THE CODE LANGUAGE OF THE MARINE CORPS

Philip Johnston, a civil engineer for the city of Los Angeles, saw the value in using the Navajo language as a code language and duly contacted Marine Corps officials at Camp Elliott near San Diego. Johnston's father had been a Presbyterian missionary on the Navajo Reservation and Johnston himself had grown up speaking Navajo. He often served as a translator for his father and in official meetings and negotiations between the Navajos and the federal government. Johnston served in France during World War I and was very interested in military affairs. In fact, a newspaper article about an army experiment with Native American radio operators during war games in Louisiana (probably a group of native

In April 1942, U.S. Marine recruiters traveled to Fort Wingate, New Mexico, to enlist 29 Navajos to serve as code talkers in the U.S. war effort. Pictured here are the 29 Navajo recruits during their swearing-in ceremony at Fort Wingate.

speakers from the 32nd Division, a Wisconsin and Michigan National Guard formation) prompted him to call upon the U.S. Marines.

The presentation of his idea to marine leadership in early 1942 was on the order of a sales pitch. He brought in a few Navajo friends and lectured his audience on the complexity of the language and how it could easily be encoded. Additionally, as early as June 1940, Navajo government officials had committed their nation to the effort against those countries that were threatening "the great liberties and benefits which we enjoy on the reservation." Johnston prepared an ethnographic document on the Navajos for the commandant of the Marine Corps in February 1942, and in April of that year, U.S. Marine recruiters went to the reservation to enlist a group of 30 men fluent in the language for the initial project. The men were signed up at the reservation boarding schools at Fort Defiance, Fort Wingate, and Shiprock. Twenty-nine of the 30 reported for duty and were sent to San Diego for basic training.[86]

BOOT CAMP AND THE CREATION OF THE CODE

Basic training in the Marine Corps is more than simply learning how to march in formation, fire a weapon, or set up a pup tent. For the most part, recruit training is, and always was, an initiation into a rather select group. Quite often it is seen as the exchange of one's personal identity for membership in a well-disciplined, very different society with its own special code of ethics and set of behaviors.

The Navajo recruits did well in boot camp but complained, as did every other marine, about the seemingly petty details of their training. One interesting anecdote that Doris Paul related in her book *The Navajo Code Talkers* was about shaving. Navajos, like many other Native Americans, generally have little facial hair. Some of the marine recruits had never shaved in their lives. One Navajo marine's drill instructor ordered him to shave simply because the Marine Corps had issued razors to all recruits. Although they may have questioned the logic of shaving nonexistent facial hair, the Navajos nevertheless graduated from boot camp and went on to infantry training. For all of them, English was a second language and few of them had any life experience beyond the reservation. That they made it through the tough regimen of boot camp attested to their determination, physical endurance, and sense of teamwork.

After receiving recruit, rifle, and infantry training, the first 29 code talkers were sent to work devising the code that would eventually be used against the Japanese in the Pacific. The group was taken to Camp Elliott near San Diego for training on the use of the various kinds of radio equipment. While at Elliott, they were ordered to encode Navajo. The first group got together and, according to Cozy Stanley Brown:

> discussed how we would do it. We decided to change the name of the airplanes, ships, and the English ABC's into the Navajo language. We did the changing. For instance, we named the airplanes "dive bombers" for *ginitsoh* (sparrow hawk), because the sparrow hawk is like an airplane—it charges downward at a very fast pace. We called the enemy *ana'l*, just like the old saying of the Navajos. The name *ana'l* also is used in the Navajo Enemy Way ceremony.[87]

The code talkers only had about two months to learn how to use the equipment and devise the code. After that, eight of the men were selected to go first to the island of New Caledonia in the Pacific to prepare for the invasion of Guadalcanal. Seventeen of their number made it to the island, while two of the original 29 remained in the United States to recruit other Navajos and instruct them in the use of the code.

From the beginning, Philip Johnston visited Camp Elliott to find out how his project was progressing. He had nothing to do with the first code, but was itching to get involved. He applied for and received permission to enlist as a U.S. Marine

---

(opposite page) After the Navajo code talkers left Fort Wingate, they traveled to Camp Elliott, near San Diego, California, where they had eight weeks not only to learn how to use radio equipment but also devise a code. Both the Navajo Reservation and the location where the Navajos took part in basic training are depicted on this map.

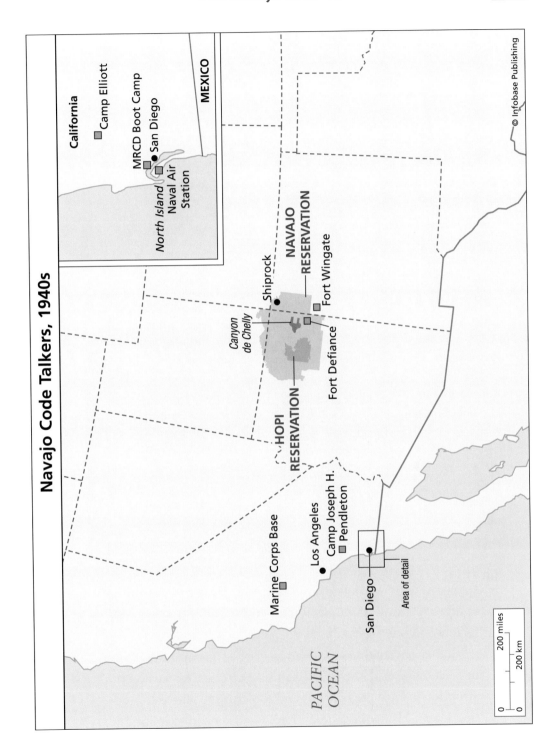

Navajo Code Talkers, 1940s

California
- Camp Elliott
- MRCD Boot Camp
- San Diego
- *North Island* Naval Air Station

MEXICO

NAVAJO RESERVATION

Shiprock
Fort Wingate
Canyon de Chelly
Fort Defiance

HOPI RESERVATION

Marine Corps Base
Los Angeles
Camp Joseph H. Pendleton

San Diego
Area of detail

PACIFIC OCEAN

200 miles
200 km
0
0

© Infobase Publishing

THE NAVAJO CODE*

During World War II, the Navajo language was used in the Pacific Theater by the U.S. armed forces to transmit secret tactical messages. Approximately 400 Navajos served in the 3rd, 4th, and 5th Divisions of the U.S. Marines and were instrumental in helping the United States achieve victory in several battles, most notably Iwo Jima. What follows is a sampling of the Navajo code, with English translation and code meaning.

Navajo Code Word/Phrase	English Translation	English Code Word or Meaning
Wol-la-chee	Ant	English Alphabet "A"
Shush	Bear	English Alphabet "B"
Moasi	Cat	English Alphabet "C"
Tabaha	Edge Water Clan	Regiment
So-na-ki	Two Stars	Major General
Atsah-besh-le-gai	Silver Eagle	Colonel
Olah-alah-ih-ni-ahi	One Gold Bar	Second Lieutenant
Gini	Chicken Hawk	Dive Bomber
Da-he-tih-hi	Hummingbird	Fighter Aircraft
Jay-sho	Buzzard	Bomber
Lo-tso	Whale	Battleship
Tsidi-ney-ye-hi	Bird Carrier	Aircraft Carrier
Chal	Frog	Amphibious

specialist with the rank of staff sergeant. Johnston was put in charge of Navajo training in October 1942 after the first code talkers had been sent overseas.

Johnston taught one newly recruited group of Navajos in December of that year. After this one class, he turned instruction over to the Navajos and took up administrative duties. Under his management, the Navajos began to refine and expand the code. It was decided that alternate terms in Navajo should be devised for the 12 most frequently used terms

Navajo Code Word/Phrase	English Translation	English Code Word or Meaning
Day-dil-jah-hi	Fire Builder	Engineer
Bih-be-al-doh-tka-ih	Three Guns	Battery
Be-al-doh-tso-lani	Many Big Guns	Artillery
Ni-ma-si	Potatoes	Hand Grenades
A-zey-al-ih	Place of Medicine	Hospital
A-knah-as-donih	Rapid Fire Gun	Machine Gun
Tal-kah Silago	Sea Soldiers	Navy
Cha-le-gai	White Caps	Sailors
Che-yehs-besi	Braided Hair	China
Cha-yes-desi	Rolled Hat	Australia
An-na-sozi	Cliff Dwelling	Fortification
Be-al-doh-cid-da-hi	Sitting Gun	Mortar
Ta-bas-dsissi	Shore Runner	Coast Guard
Bih-din-ne-dey	Put Out of Action	Casualty
Has-kay-gi-na-tah	War Chief	Commanding Officer
No-pahl-yeh-nal-tehi	Canvas Soldiers	Paratroopers
Be-sitihn	Deer Lay	Delay
Mai-he-ahgan	Fox Arm	Farm
Ne-he-mah	Our Mother	America
Gah-bih-tkeen	Rabbit Trail	Route
Lobe-ca	Fish Shell	Torpedo

* Partial list from Doris A. Paul's *The Navajo Code Talkers* (Philadelphia: Dorrance & Company, 1973), 24–29, 39–45.

in the English alphabet. The repetition of letters is a key to unlocking any code. The letter "A" in English is a vowel that appears regularly—so regularly that a code-breaker knows exactly how many are used in a common English sentence. The code-breaker then goes on to fill in the blanks based on the frequency of the terms used. Consequently, the Navajo code talkers began to use several terms for "A," including *Wol-la-chee* (ant), *Be-la-sana* (apple), and *Tse-nihi* (axe). Several terms were adopted for all the vowels and several consonants. They also expanded the code to include terms for various countries. Eventually the code contained a vocabulary of 411 terms. Those who used it on a regular basis became very fast in encoding, sending, receiving, decoding, and translating messages. It not only took a great memory to be a code talker, but also an almost unbelievable ability to use both Navajo and English correctly and quickly.

THE CODE TALKERS IN BATTLE

Additionally, the code talkers had to learn to be adaptable and innovative in combat. One of the code talkers told a story about how, on Guadalcanal, they had to have some kind of platform to steady a field radio set that had to be hand-cranked to send and receive messages. It could not be set up and cranked in the sand, and since no steady board platform was available, the Navajo marines hooked the set on a coconut tree. One of the operators could then straddle the tree and turn the crank handles. The same marine also told about their need for speed and accuracy:

> One thing we learned in school was not to be on the air longer than was absolutely necessary. We had to be careful not to repeat words in a sentence—that is, if the message had to go through more than once, we tried to say it differently every time. We were also told not to use the same word too often in a sentence, and that we had to be *accurate* the first time! If a message has to be corrected or repeated too often, you are giving the enemy a better chance to locate you. On Guadalcanal we had to move our equipment in a hurry because the [Japanese] started to shell the very spot where we were operating.[88]

Many Japanese citizens were educated in the United States. The Japanese were therefore able to use American

Navajo code talkers were instrumental in saving several U.S. combat units during World War II. However, code talkers did much more than simply transmit and receive messages; by the end of the war, they were hardened combat veterans. Here, Corporal Lloyd Oliver of the 1st Marine Division operates a field radio in July 1943.

jargon to send false messages or to confuse transmissions. A Japanese soldier who could speak English without an accent and imitate American slang could in fact call for an American artillery strike on U.S. troops. These imitations of messages came often enough to make U.S. officers wary of any plain English transmission. As a result, a frequently asked radio question was, "Have you got a Navajo?" In answer, a code talker would be put on the line. The Navajo code saved more than one American unit from being annihilated by their own comrades.

Of course, when the combat became intense, the Navajo marines simply had to put down their radio headsets and fight. They carried a variety of weapons, from standard issue M-1s to Browning automatic rifles to .30 caliber machine guns, in addition to their radio equipment. They were also pressed into service carrying stretchers. During the landings on Saipan, one code talker's assault craft was turned over about 300 yards from the beach. He tried to take off his pack but it was caught on some debris or some other equipment he was carrying. He nearly drowned, but he kept struggling through the surf to the beach. He described the experience later: "As I was coming ashore someone cut off the pack with a combat knife, and dragged me up on shore. Water was coming out of my mouth and nose; but I survived, and we found our company that night."[89]

The next morning, the same marine had to go back to the beach to get his pack. He found there the bodies of many marines who had been killed in the initial assault. He had to take another pack and a weapon from one of the bodies. At the same time, some U.S. tanks came ashore and he began to follow them inland. The Japanese zeroed in on the tanks and he was wounded by a Japanese mortar blast. For the next week, he felt as if his head had swelled up beyond normal proportions. The Navajo people traditionally have an aversion to dead bodies and graveyards. In Navajo society, highly specialized medicine people prepare the dead for burial and the burial places themselves are normally avoided. When a Navajo dies in a *hogan* (the traditional eight-sided Navajo house), the dwelling is usually abandoned and a new house is built for the other family members. Anyone who has touched or even been around the dead for a period of time must be ritually purified in special ceremonies. The Navajo marine who had to take a pack and a weapon from a dead person must have suffered emotionally in addition to being physically wounded.

Compounding the horrors of being around dead bodies on a regular basis, the terrible living conditions on the islands they invaded, and, of course, the dread of going into combat against an enemy who seemed to care little about being killed in battle, Navajo code talkers also had to be wary of their own American comrades in arms. The fact that the code was a closely guarded secret gave rise to the notion that specially assigned security agents accompanied the Navajos to check on broadcast circuits and look for misplaced scripts that the Japanese might use to decipher the code. There was also a rumor that these agents were there to prevent the Japanese from capturing the Navajos, even if it meant killing the individual code talker. Capture was a very real danger for the Navajos. As indicated by William C. Meadows's research on Comanche code talkers and code talking in general, Japanese and German linguists were studying Native American languages well before the war. Several reports and bulletins from the Washington-based Bureau of American Ethnology contained Native American word lists and grammars, and by 1944, the Japanese knew that the marines were using Navajo over the radios. The Japanese captured Joe Kieyoomia, a Navajo, and tortured him in the attempt to break the code. Kieyoomia was not a code talker and, although fluent in Navajo, could provide the Japanese with no information that they could use.[90]

But as one code talker would later relate, the bodyguards were there primarily to prevent other Americans from mistaking the Navajos for the Japanese. Toward the end of the Guadalcanal campaign, a U.S. Army unit took a Navajo code talker prisoner. The army commander sent a message to U.S. Marine headquarters that his men had captured a Japanese soldier "in Marine clothing and Marine identification tags." The man in question was identified finally as an "Indian communicator" and returned to his unit. Although the incident could have been lethal for the young Navajo, he was described as being "bored with the proceedings."

Another incident of misidentification was not boring at all. During one Japanese night attack, things got rather confusing and marines mixed with army personnel in the fight. While under fire, an army officer pulled out his .45 and grabbed a code talker, whom he thought was a Japanese infiltrator. The Navajo marine would later explain that his beard grew like that of a Japanese man. "An Anglo beard will follow the contour of the chin," he said, while his grew "straight down." The officer threatened to shoot him, but finally agreed to take the code talker to headquarters.

In another incident, a Navajo marine was in an army supply area looking for some orange juice when two soldiers confronted him. After questioning the man, an army sergeant ventured the guess that because the code talker had marine dog tags and spoke English well, he must be an American. Another soldier answered, "I don't care if he graduated from Ohio State. We're going to shoot him." The soldiers took the code talker to a marine unit, where he was identified as a communicator. After this incident, the Navajo was assigned a "bodyguard."

The mistakes continued even after Guadalcanal. On Saipan, a code talker was taking a bath in a shell hole filled with water. This time a military policeman (MP) took him prisoner and walked him back to a prisoner collection point without his clothing. The code talker's commanding officer finally identified him and he was released.[91] Luckily, either the "bodyguards" did their jobs or the code talkers were able to talk themselves out of these difficult situations, because none of them was reported to have been the victim of an on-the-spot execution.

The dangers they faced were numerous: dug-in Japanese, suicidal charges, bombing raids, snipers, mines, booby traps, as well as being mistaken for Japanese soldiers by their own comrades. Despite these dangers, they accomplished their mission and should be considered thorough professionals. The Navajo code was never broken and was a great factor in winning the war in the Pacific. Among the many marine officers who praised the code talkers was Lieutenant General R. E. Cushman, later commandant of the Marine Corps, who said, "The Navajo code talkers, of course, prevented the enemy from understanding the messages and, therefore, were of considerable value." Another, Major Howard M. Conner, stated without equivocation, "Were it not for the Navajos, the Marines would never have taken Iwo Jima!" In fact, he continued, "The entire operation was directed by Navajo code."[92]

Cozy Stanley Brown, who was with the first group of 29 code talkers, fought the Japanese in Guadalcanal, New Guinea, Bougainville, Cape Gloucester, and Peleliu. He participated in defensive battles against Japanese banzai charges and in silent night attacks on Japanese positions. On Cape Gloucester, he fought hand-to-hand with a Japanese soldier and killed him with a knife. Before the war was over, he was given a 35-day leave, during which he returned to his reservation to have an "Enemy Way" ceremony that purified him and aided him psychologically to overcome the emotional stress of experiencing that much combat. After his leave, Brown became an instructor at Camp Pendleton in California. He was there when the war ended.

Brown was interviewed for the book *Navajos in World War II*. He told his story with dignity and concluded that the war in which he sacrificed so much was necessary for the protection of his land and tradition. Most important, he told his story so that young people would know the extent of the Navajo contribution to winning the war. He said:

> The younger generations need to know the stories and lives of the older people and of the past. I hope that what I have said will be useful in telling the important things done by the Navajos in the second World War.[93]

Native Americans in the European Theater

As a result of a system of worldwide alliances and the arrogance of the foremost European dictator, Adolf Hitler, Germany mistakenly followed Japan in declaring war on the United States. It might be said that a war between the United States and Nazi Germany was a foregone conclusion. The whole of Europe had been plunged into war when the German *Wehrmacht* (army) attacked Poland in September 1939. Hitler then followed with an attack on France in 1940, a devastating air war against Great Britain, the conquest of the rest of eastern Europe, and the invasion of the Soviet Union in June 1941. Stopping Hitler's plans for world domination became the obsession of Winston Churchill, Joseph Stalin, and Franklin Roosevelt for myriad reasons, not the least of which was political self-preservation. Even before the United States entered the war as a full-fledged combatant, Roosevelt and his military advisors, chiefly General George Marshall, and Winston Churchill had agreed that Germany, more than its Axis allies Italy and Japan, was the most dangerous foe. Consequently, the Allies aimed to concentrate on defeating

Hitler first; Stalin was focused on expelling the Germans from Russian soil in any case. Money, men, and equipment would be reserved for the battle in Europe.

At the same time, Americans were eager for revenge against the Japanese. The Japanese had attacked first and had made a mockery of the international code of conduct that called for the fair treatment of prisoners of war. General MacArthur, who vowed to return to the Philippines, and Admiral Ernest King, the U.S. Navy's chief of staff, whose main concern was keeping the fleet intact in the Pacific, protested against the focus on Europe to no avail. But the British kept dragging their feet in regard to opening a western front in Europe, and so Roosevelt gave in and allowed MacArthur and King to proceed with plans to attack Guadalcanal. Still, the president severely limited the Pacific war's budget, so much so that the Guadalcanal assault, officially known as "Operation Watchtower," was called in private "Operation Shoestring."

The Soviet Union was in a battle for its very existence and Stalin was loudly calling on the United States and Great Britain to open a second front, preferably in France, to take the heat off Germany's drive into Russian territory. Roosevelt and the U.S. generals were all for opening up the second front in 1943, but Churchill and his generals again balked; they did not want to take the risk of being tossed out of the European mainland as had happened to them during the German *blitzkreig* bombing of France and Belgium in 1940. The British had their way. The first U.S. offensive would take place in North Africa against French Vichy forces in Morocco and Algeria. It was thought that since Marshal Philippe Pétain, the French dictator, was a halfhearted ally of Germany only because Hitler's forces occupied France, the conquest of Morocco would be a relatively easy proposition for the untested U.S. troops. The "real" battle in North Africa was a contest between General Bernard Montgomery's

8th British Army and the famous field marshal Erwin Rommel and his Afrika Corps.

Montgomery dealt Rommel a heavy blow at El Alamein, Egypt, in October 1942. The Afrika Corps retreated back through Libya to its Tunisia stronghold. Meanwhile, the Americans had landed, taken their objectives in Algeria and Morocco, and were making advances into Tunisia. Field Marshal Rommel decided that because the British were in a slow pursuit of him after El Alamein, he might as well deal the advancing Americans a severe setback. The Americans met the Germans at Kasserine Pass and were badly mauled. Despite that, though, Rommel failed to throw the Americans out of Tunisia. Hitler recalled him before the regrouped Americans attacked once again and hammered what was left of the Afrika Corps against the anvil of the British 8th Army. The North Africa campaign was over by March 1943. The final Axis surrender in Africa came that May.

Roosevelt and Churchill met at the Casablanca Conference in January 1943, even before the Axis forces in North Africa had been defeated. The conference turned out to be a major strategic meeting that once again delayed a direct attack on German-held France. Churchill and his generals were still against opening a second front in France that early in the war and talked Roosevelt into attacking Sicily and then mainland Italy. The Casablanca Conference led to some of the bloodiest fighting in all of World War II.

The Sicilian campaign was another amphibious assault, launched on July 10, 1943. Robert Stabler, a young man from the Omaha tribe of Nebraska, was among the first of the U.S. troops to set foot in Sicily. In fact, he volunteered to land "alone under heavy fire" to mark the beaches for the infantry landing teams in advance of the assault at Licata. Stabler's actions at Licata perhaps confirmed for his fellow soldiers the ideas and stereotypes of Native Americans as scouts and warriors.

(continues on page 90)

WHERE THEY FOUGHT IN EUROPE AND NORTH AFRICA

The 14 men and women and the Comanche code talkers who are listed on the facing page are among the thousands of Native Americans who fought in the European Theater during World War II.

1. Robert Stabler (Omaha), 3rd "Marne" Infantry Division. North Africa, Sicily, Cassino, and Anzio.
2. Hollis Stabler (Omaha), 2nd "Hell on Wheels" Armored Division, 1st Ranger Battalion, and 1st Special Forces Services. Morocco, Sicily, Anzio, and southern France.
3. Ernest Childers (Muscogee Creek), 45th "Thunderbird" Infantry Division. North Africa, Sicily, Salerno. Medal of Honor action near Oliveto, Italy.
4. Jack C. Montgomery (Cherokee), 45th "Thunderbird" Infantry Division. Sicily, Salerno, Cassino, Anzio. Medal of Honor action on the road near Padiglione, Italy.
5. Van T. Barfoot (Choctaw), 45th "Thunderbird" Infantry Division. Sicily, Salerno, Cassino, Anzio. Medal of Honor action on the road between Anzio and Rome, Italy.
6. Kent C. Ware (Kiowa), 8th Army Air Force, Great Britain. Bombing runs over France, Belgium, Holland, and Germany.
7. Edward Tinker (Osage), Strategic Air Force. Bombing runs over southern and eastern Europe.
8. William R. Fredenberg (Menominee), 9th Army Air Force. Tactical dive bombing in France.
9. Shuman Shaw (Paiute), Strategic Air Force. Southern and eastern Europe.
10. Comanche Code Talkers, 4th "Ivy" Infantry Division. Utah Beach, France, Luxembourg, Siegfried Line, Hürtgen Forest, and Battle of the Bulge.
11. Charles K. Louie (Coeur d'Alene), 82nd "All American" Airborne Division. D-Day.
12. Dave Bald Eagle (Lakota), 82nd "All American" Airborne Division. Sicily, D-Day, Battle of the Hedgerows, France.
13. McManus "Blacky" Broncho (Shoshone-Bannock), 80th "Blue Ridge" Infantry Division. Normandy, France, relief of Bastogne, and Battle of the Bulge.
14. Marcella LeBeau (Dakota), Army Nurse Corps. Liège, Belgium, and Battle of the Bulge.
15. Schlicht Billy (Choctaw), 45th "Thunderbird" Infantry Division. Italy, southern France, and Siegfried Line.

Note: Numbers correspond to numbers listed on map; participant's tribe in parentheses.

(continued from page 87)

Later, his brother Hollis wrote in his own memoirs of service in World War II that "Bob was just doing his job." Robert Stabler would continue to do his job and live up to the expectations of the Native American soldier in combat until he was killed in action at Cisterna, Italy, in early 1944. For his actions in Sicily, he was posthumously awarded the Silver Star.[94]

Among the attacking divisions under the overall command of Lieutenant General George S. Patton was the 45th "Thunderbird" Infantry, which was as close to a Native American unit as any in the U.S. Army. The 45th was made up of National Guard units from the states of Oklahoma, Colorado, New Mexico, and Arizona. All of these states had large Native American populations. Of course, by July 1943, the 45th had been made into a regular army formation and the draft had been in full swing for three years. Consequently, the division was fully integrated with personnel from places like New York, Maine, Mississippi, and Connecticut. The Sicilian campaign was particularly difficult and hindered by internal conflicts among the Allies over strategy. General Patton, with his 7th Army, wanted to land on the northern part of the island, while the British 8th Army under General Montgomery wanted to land in the south. Patton's plan would be a pincer movement toward the port of Messina, located immediately across from the Italian mainland. General Montgomery wanted both forces to land in the south with the Americans covering his flank while he moved on a narrow front to capture Messina. (Montgomery eventually won out.) When Montgomery's 8th Army became mired in a terrible battle for the mountainous region of the island, Patton swiftly moved north, taking the large city of Palermo, and finally reached Messina in August 1943. Landing the Americans in the south, however, cost the Allies time. Four German divisions were allowed to transship their personnel and equipment from Messina to Italy. These divisions would later play a large roll in challenging the American and British invasion of mainland Italy.[95]

Under Fascist dictator Benito Mussolini, Italy had paid a terrible price in the war. In addition to its losses in battle deaths, nearly 600,000 Italian soldiers were taken prisoner. The Soviet Union had taken an entire Italian army of 200,000 and the Americans and British captured another 350,000 Italian soldiers in North Africa alone. The Allies' seizure of Sicily was the last straw. On July 25, just 15 days after the landings on Sicily, the Fascist Grand Council requested Mussolini's resignation as the prime minister of Italy. King Victor Emmanuel summoned Mussolini to the royal palace and had him arrested, whereupon the king assumed control of all Italian armed forces and appointed General Pietro Badoglio as prime minister. Although the new government informed the Germans that Italy would remain in the war, it secretly began peace talks with the Allies. Hitler, suspecting such a scenario, ordered more German troops to prepare for the defense of Italy against further Allied landings. On September 8, 1943, Italy officially surrendered. Five days before Montgomery's 8th Army landed at Reggio di Calabria and on the same day that Italy officially surrendered, General Dwight D. Eisenhower, commander of the Allied forces in Europe, announced that the Americans would assault Salerno, near Naples. The Italian campaign was underway.

The battle for the Italian boot raged from 1943 to 1945 and made for some of the bloodiest fighting in the entire war. It was also the campaign that saw some of the most heroic episodes of combat in World War II. Three Native American soldiers from the 45th Division won Congressional Medals of Honor in Italy in three separate battles.

The first was Lieutenant Ernest Childers, a Muscogee Creek from Broken Arrow, Oklahoma. On September 22, 1943, Childers was leading an advance party of eight other men near Oliveto, Italy, when several German machine-gun

Lieutenant Ernest Childers (Muscogee Creek) was the first of three Native Americans from the 45th Infantry Division of the U.S. Army to be presented with the Congressional Medal of Honor for his valor in action. Childers, who passed away in March 2005, is pictured here with General Jacob L. Devers in July 1944, shortly after he was awarded the medal.

nests opened up on them. Despite a painful broken instep, Childers ordered his men to lay down suppressive fire while he advanced alone toward the nearest machine-gun nest. Two German snipers fired on him from a house near the action. He was able to kill both snipers and moved behind two of the machine-gun nests. He killed the soldiers occupying the nearest one and moved on to the next. After finishing off this German position, he moved toward the house and single-handedly captured an enemy mortar observer who had been calling down a number of mortar rounds on the Americans.

The next "Thunderbird" to win the Congressional Medal of Honor was Lieutenant Jack C. Montgomery, a Cherokee from the tiny town of Long, Oklahoma. Montgomery was in command of an infantry company in a defensive position near Padiglione, Italy. On February 22, 1944, the Germans took up position immediately opposite that of Montgomery. The nearest German position consisted of four machine-gun nests and a mortar emplacement. Taking an M-1 rifle and several grenades, Montgomery advanced on the German position and wiped it out. He returned to his company and called in an artillery strike on the Germans. When he found out that a second German position had not been knocked out by the artillery, he took an M-1 carbine and attacked it alone. He killed three Germans and seven surrendered to him. He continued to work his way up a hill toward a house. Montgomery attacked the house in the face of a strong defense and managed to kill and capture several enemy soldiers. At the end of his actions that day, he had attacked three enemy positions and accounted for 11 enemy dead, 32 prisoners, and an unknown number of wounded. Later that day, he was seriously wounded and had to be evacuated.

Van T. Barfoot, a Choctaw from Carthage, Mississippi, was a lieutenant in charge of a platoon advancing along the road from the Anzio beachhead to Rome. During a firefight on May 23, 1944, Barfoot charged two German machine-gun nests, killing several enemy soldiers and taking 17 prisoners. The Germans countered with a tank assault. Barfoot took up a bazooka and single-handedly repelled the tanks. He went on to destroy a German artillery piece and save two wounded

Americans, carrying them back to the safety of his own lines while suffering from wounds of his own.

The battle for Italy was a costly and gory crawl up the peninsula. The Allies made four major amphibious landings in Italy. The first came with the crossing of the Strait of Messina from Sicily to Reggio on the toe of the Italian boot on September 3, 1943. Six days later, the Allies made two parallel landings at Salerno and Paranto, in the eastern and western parts of the country, respectively. After those two assaults, the Allies proceeded northeast toward a heavily fortified German defensive position known as the Gustav Line, which stretched across the breadth of Italy. The attack on the Gustav Line led to the terrible battle of Cassino between January and May 1944. In order to flank the Gustav Line and force a break that would lead to the capture of Rome, the Americans made another amphibious landing at Anzio on January 22. After two months of being held down on the beaches at Anzio, the Americans were finally able to break out toward the capital. Rome fell on June 4. From then on the Allies became preoccupied with Operation Overlord in France and the Italian campaign ground to a near standstill on the German Gothic Line that ran across Italy once again. The Gothic Line was not breached until late 1944.[96, 97]

THE AIR WAR

After the British Royal Air Force had beaten off the German attempt to bomb the United Kingdom into submission in 1940 and 1941, the air ministry began to retaliate. Germany continued to bomb various British targets during the first years of the war, particularly London. The *blitz*, as it was called, was really a terror campaign instituted to demoralize the British rather than destroy their industrial ability to continue the war. Off shore, the British were engaged in a battle for the Atlantic as well. German U-boats, organized into "wolf packs," were sinking Allied ships on a regular basis. It would not be until British and American airpower provided cover for the convoys—in the form of aircraft flying off the new escort carriers—that the strength of the wolf packs began to diminish.

Meanwhile, Great Britain launched an air campaign against Germany. At first the British bombers were mauled by German interceptors, but then the British began to bomb German cities at night. The British always denied that the night bombing was in fact simply a terror tactic. They rationalized the bombing as an attempt to destroy German industry by "de-housing" German workers. Presumably, if workers' homes were destroyed, the workers themselves would be so demoralized they would cease to be as productive as they were before. In fact, the opposite turned out to be true.

U.S. bombers and their crews began arriving in Great Britain in 1942. Organized as the 8th Air Force, its commanders perceived the bombing campaign against Germany in a different way. Flying B-17s, the Americans thought that they could carry out daylight precision bombing raids on German industrial targets. The B-17s were called "Flying Fortresses" because they bristled with a dozen .50 caliber machine guns. If they flew in formation, they could supposedly defend themselves against German interceptor attacks. The B-17s also carried a very accurate bombsight. After the 1943 Casablanca Conference between Churchill and Roosevelt, the daytime American bombing campaign was to be coordinated with the British bombing at night.[98, 99]

Kent C. Ware, a Kiowa from Oklahoma, was a tech sergeant who flew the daylight bombing raids in a B-17. Admittedly proud of the aircraft he flew in and, as a gunner, proud of his "kills" of German interceptors, he also admitted that as the war progressed the bombing became more and more difficult. German fighters were improving and, since German Air Force and Army troops occupied France, Belgium, Holland, and Denmark, they had antiaircraft emplacements all along the air corridors leading to the German homeland and industrial areas. Early in the air war, there were no long-range

Allied fighters and so the bombers had to go it alone. Fire from the German antiaircraft guns was always heavy both to and from the targets. Sergeant Ware won the Air Medal with two oak leaf clusters (a total of three awards) and after he was wounded in action received the Purple Heart medal. Sergeant Ware was once asked which U.S. bomber he preferred: the B-17 or the B-24. Without hesitation he answered, "You hit one B-24, four of them fall, I'll take the 17."[100]

The reasons that Sergeant Ware gave for the heavy losses of U.S. bombers during the air war in Europe was the lack of long-range fighter escorts and the fact that the British bombing plan was ineffective. The German workers were simply not giving up. In fact, their morale could not have been higher. Their losses and the thousands of German civilians killed in the bombing raids only seemed to bolster their resolve to fight. But there was something equally wrong with the American precision bombing campaign. The Americans were suffering heavy losses in planes and personnel due to the lack of fighter escorts and the heavy attacks from anti-aircraft fire, only to find that the high-grade steel of German machinery was almost impervious to high explosives.

As the U.S. planes were shot down, the numbers of American prisoners of war multiplied. General Clarence Tinker's nephew, Major Edward Tinker, was himself shot down over Bulgaria. The Germans held him until 1945, when the Soviets liberated his prison camp. Lieutenant Frank Paisano from Laguna Pueblo, New Mexico, was a prisoner of the Germans after his bomber was shot down. An Osage from Oklahoma like the Tinkers, Gilmore C. Daniels had actually joined the Royal Canadian Air Force early in the war. Flying with the Canadians, he was shot down and held in a German prisoner of war camp for four years.[101] It was not until 1944, when the P-51 Mustang fighter appeared in force and when the Normandy invasion drew the German air forces to France, that the U.S. bombing campaign stopped suffering great losses.

By then, too, the bombing had shifted from Germany to France, a much closer target.

The nation's highest aviation award and second-highest medal, next to the Congressional Medal of Honor, is the Distinguished Flying Cross. Thirty Native Americans were awarded this medal for their service in the air war. One cross went to Lieutenant William R. Fredenberg, a Menominee from Wisconsin, who, as a dive-bomber pilot over France, destroyed three trains carrying supplies to the German divisions there and strafed enemy installations under heavy antiaircraft fire until his ammunition ran out. Another was Sergeant Shuman Shaw, who served as a tail gunner aboard a B-24 on a bombing run over Budapest, Hungary. Shaw, a Paiute from California, personally shot down two German fighters attacking his airplane and had a hand in destroying three more. All together, Shaw was awarded a Distinguished Flying Cross, the Air Medal with three oak leaf clusters, a Presidential Unit Citation, and a Purple Heart with an oak leaf cluster. If for no other reason, the American air war against Germany should be remembered as a gallant and bloody sacrifice.[102]

THE DRIVE AGAINST GERMANY

The last American front that opened against Germany began with Operation Overlord. The Americans, British, Canadians, Free French, and Free Polish troops hit the beaches of Normandy, France, on June 6, 1944. This grand undertaking was aimed specifically at securing a large operational land base from which the Allies could drive north and east into the heart of Germany. It would be known forever simply as D-Day.

Although very large in scale, the overall plan for D-Day was relatively simple. On the night of June 5 to 6, three airborne divisions, the American 82nd and 101st and the British 6th, would parachute behind the German beach defenses. They would then secure the far flanks of the main attack and

On June 6, 1944, U.S. troops stormed the beaches of Normandy, France, during D-Day. Several Native Americans, including Charles K. Louie (Coeur d'Alene) and Dave Bald Eagle (Cheyenne River Sioux), took part in the D-Day operations.

capture roads and bridges for the Allied infantry and armor divisions to use while penetrating deep into the Normandy countryside. On the morning of June 6, the Allied assault would take place on five designated beaches, from west to east "Utah," "Omaha," "Gold," "Juno," and "Sword." Utah and Omaha beaches were the American zones of attack, with the U.S. 4th landing at Utah to link up with the 82nd and 101st Airborne divisions inland. Omaha Beach was to be attacked by the U.S. 29th and 1st infantry divisions. The British 50th and 7th armored were to hit Gold Beach, while the 3rd Canadian and the 3rd British infantry divisions assaulted Juno and Sword beaches, respectively. The American 2nd Ranger Battalion made a separate landing at Pointe-du-Hoc between

Utah and Omaha beaches to scale an imposing cliff in order to knock out the German artillery batteries that would have endangered the entire operation.[103, 104]

The U.S. paratroopers almost met with disaster from the very outset of D-Day. The 82nd and 101st divisions were scattered throughout their drop zones. Members of both divisions became mixed up and were left wandering all over the countryside. Some were actually dropped in the middle of towns, most notably Sainte Mère Église, where the Germans shot them while still in the air and left their bodies hanging from rooftops, church spires, and lampposts. Several of the aircraft carrying the troops were shot down in a hail of antiaircraft fire. One Native American, Charles K. Louie with the 82nd, was lost in this manner. A member of the Coeur d'Alene tribe of Idaho, Louie is still remembered by his people as a gallant warrior in the oldest, most traditional sense of the word.[105]

Another Native American member of the 82nd who parachuted into Normandy that night was Chief Dave Bald Eagle of the Cheyenne River Sioux. Bald Eagle joined the U.S. Army in 1939, signing up with the 4th U.S. Cavalry. When the cavalry was mechanized, or disbanded, Bald Eagle went to the infantry. He was about to be discharged when World War II began. In need of veteran soldiers, his commanders asked him to reenlist. He did so and eventually was sent to airborne training. Bald Eagle made the first American parachute and glider drops in the European Theater of the war, landing in Sicily and Salerno in 1943. He then made the jump into Normandy and fought for 33 days before being severely wounded. He was one of the 5,245 paratroopers who were killed, wounded, or declared missing during Operation Overlord.[106]

On June 7, the landings went on as scheduled. The British and Canadian divisions moved inland briskly and secured their first objectives. The American divisions assigned to Omaha Beach, however, were immediately pinned down in an appalling scene of carnage, the vastness of which has not been matched by any other amphibious assault. In a single day, more than 1,000 soldiers were killed on Omaha Beach; the casualties there made up the vast majority of those suffered by the U.S. Army on D-Day.

At dawn on June 6, the 13 members of the Comanche code talkers landed under fire on Utah Beach. As part of the 4th "Ivy" Infantry Division, the men took part in the battles of the Hedgerows, the Bulge, Paris, Hürtgen Forest, and Siegfried Line. As one person remarked, the Comanches literally "walked and fought from Utah Beach to Czechoslovakia in less than a year." From the first day of the landings, the Americans had been tied down in a battle for the *bocage*, or hedgerow, country in Normandy. After the Americans captured the town of Saint-Lô, the allied commander, General Eisenhower, launched Operation Cobra. The operation began on July 24 from Saint-Lô and resulted in the anticipated charge across France led by General George S. Patton's 3rd Army.[107]

The drive across France led to the liberation of the French capital of Paris, as well as the nations of Luxembourg and Belgium. The drive very nearly resulted in the capture of Germany's entire Army Group B in the battle of the Argentan-Falaise Gap in mid-August 1944. In June, the Soviet Union had launched a massive military campaign known as Operation Bagration in the east. Within a span of less than two months, the Red Army had driven the Germans completely out of Russia, marched to the Vistula River in Poland, and had liberated Romania. When the Americans began landings in southern France on August 15—Operation Anvil/Dragoon—the Germans were dealing with the trauma of defeat on every front. With Anvil/Dragoon, the 7th Army under General Alexander Patch Jr., ensured the German downfall in France.

Hollis Stabler, the Omaha Indian soldier who had earlier lost his brother in Italy, took part in Anvil/Dragoon as part of a special forces unit assigned the duty of taking Port Cros, an island just off the coast of France. Stabler's unit landed in an inflatable rubber craft that had been towed in by a British torpedo boat. The fight for the island lasted for two days. Several days later, Stabler was carrying one of his platoon's machine guns in the drive on the town of Grasse. While marching near a stream toward the village, a German machine gunner opened up on his men. Stabler set up his gun and

> [f]ired an entire belt at that target. Soon, a white flag appeared on a stick. We packed up and crossed the stream. Four or five young Germans stood over there, lined up, about fifteen or sixteen years old, it seemed. I could also see a couple of soldiers lying on the ground in the bushes. My shooting had been good. It was still payback for my brother, Bob.[108]

The youth of the German soldiers Stabler described indicated that Germany was running short of seasoned veterans and that the Nazi high command was desperate enough to send untested teenagers to the battlefront.

The two Allied assaults in France joined together in mid-September and continued the drive toward Germany. Only six days after the linkage between Patton's 3rd Army out of Normandy and Patch's 7th Army from the south, British General Montgomery launched Operation Market/Garden in the attempt to take the Dutch city of Arnhem and cross the Rhine River into Germany itself. The American 82nd and 101st Airborne divisions took part in the failed attempt. Although the "Market" part of the assault actually made it into German territory, the "Garden" units ultimately had to withdraw or be cut off by two SS tank divisions operating in the area.[109]

The U.S. 4th Division, to which the Comanche code talkers belonged, fared much better in the attempt to cross into the heart of Germany. The division and the code talkers, who were engaged in laying telephone wire to the spearhead units, entered Germany on September 11, 1944. Unfortunately, the German defenses, known as the Siegfried Line, held fast and the 4th Division's advance was stopped cold. The Siegfried Line, or the West Wall, was a three-mile deep series of pillboxes, troop shelters, command posts, and antitank obstacles known as "Dragon's Teeth"—hardened cement pyramids that made the passage of U.S. armored vehicles virtually impossible.[110, 111]

By the autumn, the whole American offensive into Germany was grinding to a halt due to several factors. Some of the German defenses, like the Siegfried Line, were stronger than anticipated. Market/Garden had failed largely because it was poorly timed. In addition, the Allied advance had been so rapid, particularly that of the 3rd and 7th Armies, that their supply lines were dangerously close to being overextended. The halt, although made miserable by German artillery and bad weather, at least allowed some respite to the fierce, very close combat. It also gave Hitler the breathing space he needed to plan a counterattack.

In early November, the 4th Division made another attempt to carry the offensive into Germany by way of Hürtgen Forest on the border of Belgium and Germany. Deep in the forest, the Comanche code talkers were laying telephone lines to the forward infantry positions. Dismal weather and the cold of a November snowfall added to the gloomy atmosphere. And then the German shells began to plunge through the trees. Code talker Forrest Kassanavoid later described the fighting in Hürtgen Forest:

> [I]t was dangerous for us because a lot of these artillery shells that would hit, would knock these [tree] limbs off, and you could never tell whether you was going to get hit with one of those things. And of course, that was a hell of

a fight over there in the Hürtgen Forest. . . . It was thick with trees and the Germans would use tree burst artillery shells. The splinters off the trees could kill you. It was like a meat grinder. They'd send in troops and they'd just get chewed up.[112]

THE BATTLE OF THE BULGE

As winter began to descend on Europe in late 1944, many of the frontline U.S. troops were withdrawn to rear areas for much-needed rest. The famous 101st Airborne, which parachuted behind enemy lines on D-Day, was put into a defensive perimeter around the town of Bastogne, Belgium. The 4th Infantry, which landed on D-Day at Utah Beach, was sent to Luxembourg. Patton's 3rd Army was stopped in its well-worn tank tracks as a result of a supply shortage, as was Patch's 7th Army operating to the south.

The German high command, in the meantime, was planning a bold offensive intended to split the Allied front in half and eventually protect Antwerp, the principal Belgian seaport, from falling out of German hands. The attack would be made through the Ardennes, a heavily forested, mountainous region on the German-Belgian border. The Germans had used the Ardennes to cover their attacks on Belgium and France in 1914 and in 1940. They evidently thought that the Ardennes would afford them cover once again in late 1944. And, because Hitler concentrated three divisions, two of them tank divisions, against only four tired or untested U.S. divisions in Luxembourg and eastern Belgium, the Germans gained immediate success. The four U.S. divisions were the 4th "Ivy" (the formation to which the Comanche code talkers belonged), the 28th "Keystone," the 106th Infantry, and the 9th Armored. Combined, the 4th and the 28th had suffered more than 9,000 casualties in the Hürtgen Forest; the 106th and the 9th Armored were entirely new to combat.

The German attacking armies drove through Luxembourg and deep into Belgium on December 16. In the center,
the German spearheads quickly sliced through the weakened
28th and the 106th. The forward elements of the 106th were
completely surrounded. In the south, the tough 4th Infantry
resisted with little else than the bullets in their rifles and their
own courage. The 4th actually held up the German advance
for a while—time enough for General Omar Bradley, along
with generals Eisenhower and Patton, to work out plans for a
counterattack. Unfortunately, the operation could not be put
into operation before one of the German tank divisions took
the key crossroads at Saint Vith in Belgium and the other tank
division had surrounded the 101st Airborne at Bastogne. One
of the greatest problems with organizing an Allied counter-
stroke was the overcast weather, which precluded any and all
air operations, including simple observation flights.

The Allied plan to counter the German advances called
upon British general Bernard Montgomery to put his 28th
Army Group, which included the veteran American 82nd Airborne and 2nd Armored divisions, into defensive positions
guarding the approaches to Antwerp. Patton's 3rd Army was
designated to pull out of its attack on Germany's West Wall,
turn 90 degrees, and drive northward through Luxembourg
and into Belgium to attack the southern flank of the German
spearheads. The ultimate goals of the attack were to relieve
Bastogne and drive the Germans out of Saint Vith.[113]

A Shoshone-Bannock from Fort Hall Reservation in
Idaho, McManus "Blacky" Broncho was with the 80th "Blue
Ridge" Division, one of the leading elements in the relief
of the 101st Airborne at Bastogne in December 1944. As a
medic, Broncho was charged with the immediate stabilization of the wounded so that they could be evacuated to rear
area aid stations and hospitals. The 80th Division's attack on
the German army units besieging Bastogne was met with

stout resistance. Broncho's platoon spearheaded the attack, but had encountered heavy enemy fire from only 300 yards distant. Broncho spotted his wounded squad leader and crawled 100 yards under heavy German fire to treat him. He treated his commander and pulled him back the 100 yards to his own lines. When he returned, he undertook the stabilization of another wounded man even though his finger had grown numb in the below-zero temperature. For his gallantry in saving the two men, "Blacky" Broncho was awarded the Bronze Star Medal with Combat V.[114]

Waiting in a Liège, Belgium, hospital to treat the wounded from Bastogne and Saint Vith was 24-year-old Marcella LeBeau, a Lakota from Cheyenne River Reservation in South Dakota. LeBeau was a nurse who first served with the Army Nurse Corps' 76th General Hospital in Minster, England. She was among the first to treat the wounded from the Normandy landings in June 1944. After the Allies pushed into Belgium, LeBeau was sent to France only to be transferred to Liège, in time to treat the wounded from the Battle of the Bulge. Liège is situated immediately to the north of where the main German thrusts took place. Forty years after her World War II experience, the French government honored LeBeau with the Knight of the Legion of Honor medal for her service in northern France and in the Ardennes. In her own words: "It was one of my greatest privileges and honor to have cared for those soldiers."[115]

By the day after Christmas 1944, the Allied commanders understood that the German attack had slowed enough to launch another campaign from the north. General Montgomery's army group began an assault on January 3, 1945. The 82nd Airborne and the British 1st Airborne drove into the German center on January 13, pushing the tank division back to their jumping-off positions. By January 18, the Allies restored their previous front. The Battle of the Bulge was costly. The Allies lost 19,000 killed in action. However, Hitler's offensive cost Germany even more—more than 100,000 German soldiers were killed in the battle.[116]

THE FALL OF ADOLF HITLER

When the German Ardennes offensive collapsed, General Eisenhower renewed the attack on the German border. Eisenhower had decided to attack on a broad front rather than attempt to pierce the German border in one or two places in narrow attacks. Consequently, the Allied attacks battered the lines again and again in the months following the Battle of the Bulge. Winter slowed American progress, but in the east the Soviet Union was taking giant strides against the Nazis. By February 1945, Soviet marshals Georgi Zhukov and Ivan Konev had recaptured all of the territory lost since 1941, swept through the Balkans and Poland, and stood poised with their army groups on the Oder River, ready to pounce on the German capital of Berlin.[117]

The steady pounding of the West Wall defenses yielded several breakthroughs. The first important, but costly, penetration of the Siegfried Line occurred on March 17, 1945, near Nieder-Wurzbach, Germany. Once again, the 180th Regiment of the 45th Division was in the thick of the fighting. Lieutenant Schlicht Billy, an Oklahoma Choctaw with the "Thunderbirds," who received a battlefield commission and served as a code talker, breached the "Dragon's Teeth." With four members of his platoon, he captured a German pillbox and killed four defenders. Then Billy and his men were pinned down. He appealed to his immediate commander, Captain Jack Treadwell, for help. Treadwell, in turn, organized several full-on assaults in the attempt to relieve Billy. The next day, Treadwell's repeated attacks resulted in the capture of several more pillboxes and the exploitation of the opening by U.S. troops. For their actions, Treadwell received the Congressional Medal of Honor and Billy, who was severely wounded in the fight, was awarded the Silver Star and the Purple Heart.[118]

Eventually, several bridgeheads were captured along the Rhine River. The Allies spread out across western Germany and one by one the cities began to fall. By April 1, the Americans had encircled the Ruhr Valley, the center of German industrial production. During that same month, the Red Army laid siege to Berlin. The war was all but over. The German armies had pulled back into their homeland. Soon, the German commanders were sending old men and young boys to the front to fill in the ranks of the depleted German divisions. Hitler and his general staff had taken refuge in his Berlin bunker dug directly under the Chancellery, the seat of the German state. With Soviet artillery raining all around his concrete and steel haven, and without the ability to call up more troops to protect himself, Hitler decided to commit suicide. On April 30, 1945, *Po'sa taiboo,* or "Crazy White Man," in the Comanche code, bit down on a cyanide pill and simultaneously shot himself in the head. Eight days later, the German armed forces surrendered unconditionally to American, British, Russian, and French commanders. V-E Day (for Victory in Europe) was declared in the United States on May 8, 1945.

The Comanche Code Talkers

DURING WORLD WAR I, THE U.S. ARMY WAS, AS WERE all of the combatants, deeply concerned with securing its methods of communication. Radios at the time were unreliable and fragile, and thus hardly useful in trench warfare. Wireless telegraphic messages had to be translated from dots and dashes to written word for the commanders and soldiers in the field. The most useful form of communication, since two parties could talk directly with one another, was the telephone. The problem with the telephone, as well as with the telegraph, was that enemy bombardments cut wires, even those that had been laid deeply underground. The enemy could also tap into these lines and easily listen to orders for troop movements, calls for artillery barrages, and discussions regarding attack plans. For the most part, men called "runners" handled communications between the generals in the rear, the artillery units, and the troops in the front trenches. Runners had the dangerous mission of moving around the trenches and in "no man's land" carrying handwritten messages. But these runners could be killed on a mission or taken prisoner. Signals intelligence during World War I was unreliable at best.

Encoding messages over telephone and telegraph wires was the best way to avoid the interception of signals between commanders and combat units. Although coding provided for some security, it also prevented messages from being read instantaneously or, in military terminology, in "real time." Decoding and encoding took time, which was often in short supply on the battlefield. A code that could be deciphered instantly was necessary. Because there were several Native Americans who spoke their own languages in the ranks, it was thought that the simple use of two Native Americans who spoke the same language could solve the problem of finding an unbreakable, easily transmittable code. What the American command did not realize at first was that all the Germans had to do to understand these signals was to find a scholar who spoke one of these languages or, better yet, capture a speaker of one of the languages and force him to translate the intercepted messages instantaneously. The solution to this problem was to encode a native language, because they were not easily understood in the first place and, if turned into a code, could not easily be deciphered even by a speaker of the language. There was a fairly significant number of Choctaws in the trenches who were fluent in their language to the point that together they could come up with a code. Because of this, they became the primary Native American code talkers of World War I.

The U.S. Army kept the basic idea underlying the use of Native American code talking in mind during the effort to modernize immediately prior to America's entrance into World War II. Additionally, the U.S. Army's North African and European campaigns were amphibious operations, requiring the same speedy, synchronized, and secure communications that the Marine Corps required in the Pacific. But the amphibious operations in Europe were actually secondary concerns; the U.S. Army had formed its special code-talking unit more than a year before the Marine Corps began recruiting Navajos to develop a code language. The army, concerned as it was with absolute security, enlisted the aid of the Comanche language, which was spoken by far fewer people than was Navajo. While the number of Navajo code talkers reached well more than 400, Comanche code talking was limited to a group of 17 men.

BASIC TRAINING AND THE DEVELOPMENT OF THE COMANCHE CODE

Although there were Comanches in the U.S. Army at the time, the officers in charge of developing the code-talker unit thought it best to train new recruits from the outset of their military service. Army recruiters were sent to western Oklahoma during December 1940 and January 1941 to look specifically for Comanches fluent in their own language. They found the 17 men relatively easily. At the time, practically every Comanche was a fluent speaker. An alphabet, or standard written form, had not yet been tailored to the language, however, and the army was counting on that fact to make Comanche even less decipherable than other Native American languages.

U.S. Army officials knew of several German attempts to learn a number of Native American languages during the 1930s. These German efforts may have been brought forth based on the knowledge that Indian languages were used as code against Germany during World War I. They may also have stemmed from a widespread German interest in Native Americans and their culture in the period. Hitler himself was said to be an admirer of the works of Karl May, a German novelist who created stories about western Americana featuring the frontiersman Old Shatterhand and his Indian companion Winnetou.[119] In any case, the German linguistic anthropologist Gunter Wagner did fieldwork among the Comanches in

1932 and a group of German "students" appeared in 1939 at a German missionary church near Indiahoma, Oklahoma, deep in the heart of Comanche country. The FBI, suspecting that the members of this group, all of whom were much older than most students, were guilty of espionage, arrested them. None were seen again in Indiahoma.[120]

The Comanche recruits were made part of the 4th Signal Company of the 4th "Ivy" Motorized Infantry Division located at Fort Benning, Georgia. To the great surprise of their drill instructors and officers, the Comanche code talkers took everything about recruit training in stride and knew much more about the military than anyone gave them credit for. All except one of the code talkers had gone to Indian boarding schools. A U.S. Army officer, Richard Henry Pratt, founded the Indian boarding school system in the United States. In the late nineteenth century, when the boarding schools began receiving students, the curriculum and the disciplinary system were designed to force each student to turn his or her back on native cultures and adopt Western dress, religion, political orientations, philosophies, customs, and mannerisms. Hence, the use of Native American languages at these schools was strictly forbidden and all manner of punishments, from whipping to kneeling on broomsticks to scrubbing floors with toothbrushes, were devised to stop the children from speaking their own languages. The irony of their experience in the boarding schools and what the army wanted of them was not lost on the Comanche code talkers. As one code talker explained:

> You got punished for talking Indian. So when we see them [boarding school teachers or officials], when we're talking Indian, we hush-up real quick. Like I say, they was always trying to make little white boys out of us. But still, when Hitler started kicking around, they was looking for Indians,

and they come back to us and asked us to use our language for that special unit, to use to send messages.[121]

Try as they did, the boarding schools were unable to break the Comanches of speaking their language. When they were on vacation during the summer and the Christmas season, they returned to their families in western Oklahoma. At the time, nearly all of the Comanche people were using the language in the home and were probably almost fully fluent. Because of this, the students needed to use Comanche simply to speak to their relatives. The U.S. government had a long way to go to eradicate the Comanche language, despite the intolerance of it in the boarding schools.

In 1879, Richard Henry Pratt became the superintendent of Carlisle Indian School in Pennsylvania. During the Civil War, Pratt had risen in rank from private to major. He stayed in the service and fought tribes, including the Comanche, on the Southern Plains. He was also the warden of the prison in Fort Marion, Florida, that incarcerated the leaders of the tribes for making war on the United States. It may well be that Pratt, the warden turned Indian educator, patterned the boarding school on military training, most notably the Prussian Regimental Schools of the period. Whatever the case, the Indian boarding schools instructed students, both boys and girls, in close-order drill so that they could be marched to their classes. In addition, they imposed a rigorous, barracks-style orderliness to the student dormitories.

Because of their boarding school experience, the Comanche code talkers actually had a fairly easy time at boot camp. Their drill sergeants found that they understood all of the commands of close-order drill and could execute various commands quickly and easily. When the drill sergeant appeared in the barracks on their first morning of training, he arrived expecting to instruct the Comanches on how to make

Although boarding schools such as Carlisle Indian School, in Carlisle, Pennsylvania, attempted to stop Native American children from speaking their respective languages, their efforts often proved fruitless. Here, six boys stand at the front of a classroom at the boarding school in 1901.

up a military bunk. He discovered that they had already done so. Said one code talker about the incident:

> We really had him going. He just scratched his head, he couldn't figure it out. He reached in his pocket and pulled out a quarter and throwed it on the bed and it just jumped right back at him. He said, "There's something wrong here. You guys aren't supposed to know all this."[122]

The Comanches kept their barracks spotless and were meticulous dressers when it came to putting on their uniforms. They knew how to spit-polish, and their shoes, boots, brass buckles, and insignia were shined to a bright finish. Having grown up hunting game in rural Oklahoma, they were well versed in the use of firearms. The rifles they were issued in recruit training were simply military versions of the same weapons they used hunting deer. Needless to say, basic military training was not difficult for them. In fact, due to their prior knowledge of basic military systems, procedures, and customs, the U.S. Army reduced their initial training from six to two weeks. They were able to start their training on the army's communications technology and develop the Comanche code faster than expected.

The training in the various kinds of communications devices—handheld radios (walkie-talkies); larger hand-cranked, two-man radios; wireless telegraphy; and telephones—was also relatively easy for the code talkers. They caught on quickly and were soon laying ground wire on par with veteran wiremen. The code they devised was also quickly developed and brilliant. They first got a list from their officers of military terms for different weapons, airplanes, and formations. Then they devised a terminology that was completely new but devised from Comanche expressions. As historian William C. Meadows explained:

> These "coded" terms were not intelligible to other non-code-talker-trained Comanche servicemen and were used largely as nouns inserted into regular noncoded Comanche sentences. Coded terms were thus used only in sending messages and not in everyday language. While most of each message sent was spoken in everyday Comanche language, the numerous insertions of specially coded military terms made it impossible for anyone not trained in the code to understand.[123]

Training and encoding progressed so rapidly that the code talkers had time for several other activities before leaving for duty. They once again borrowed from their boarding school experience and dominated the 4th Signal Company's boxing team. The Comanche pugilists filled eight of the nine weight classes on the team, as well as the job of trainer. They also participated in public-relations events. They all knew the Comanche war dance songs and were given money to buy some cowhide to make a drum. A few requested that their relatives send their dance regalia. They gave performances of traditional Comanche dancing and singing in and around Fort Benning throughout 1942 and most of 1943.

GOING TO WAR

In late 1943, training picked up and the 4th Division was notified that it would be shipped to the European Theater to fight the Germans. They were sent to several staging areas and finally to Fort Dix, New Jersey, where three members of their group were discharged from the U.S. Army. The 14 code talkers left shipped out for England in January 1944.

The 4th Division went through four months of rigorous training in preparation for Operation Overlord, the assault on Hitler's Atlantic Wall. One of the code talkers, Morris Sunrise, was transferred just before D-Day and so the number of Comanche code talkers in the 4th Signal Company dropped to 13. The division was set to land at Utah Beach in Normandy on D-Day, June 6, 1944. Luckily they survived the most infamous training disaster of the war. The 4th Division was scheduled to undergo amphibious landing exercises the night of April 27 to 28, 1944, when various problems arose. Operation Tiger, as the exercise was called, was delayed because of mistimed ship crossings and jammed embarkation points. A German U-boat slipped into the area and torpedoed two U.S. landing ships, killing 749 soldiers and sailors.

Compared to the D-Day assault on Omaha Beach, which has been described as a "bloodbath," the landings at Utah Beach went smoothly. Brigadier General Theodore Roosevelt,

THE COMANCHE CODE*

Like Navajo, the Comanche language was used by the U.S. armed forces to transmit secret tactical messages during World War II. However, because the Navajo language was used in Europe during World War I, it was feared that the Germans would be able to decipher the Navajo code. The Germans, however, were unfamiliar with the Comanche language, so the U.S. Army recruited 17 Comanches to transmit messages during the war effort. Members of the 4th Signal Company, the Comanches were particularly instrumental during D-Day, when the Allies began the Normandy invasion. What follows is a sampling of the Comanche code, with English translation and code meaning.

Comanche Code Word/Phrase	English Translation	English Code Word or Meaning
Numurekwa'etuu	Comanche Speaker	Code Talker
Paraiboo'puhk-cute-nah	Chief Location	Command Post
Waha tatsunuupi nakohpoona	Two Star Branded	Major General
Piahuutsu'	Big Bird	Colonel
Ekapuhihwitu	Red Metal	Major
Waha nakohpoo	Two Brands	Captain
Sumu nakohpoo	One Brand	Lieutenant
Pahi nakohpoo	Three Brands	Sergeant
Waha navoona	Two Marks	Corporal
Sumu navoona	One Mark	Private First Class
Taawohonuu	Our Enemies	Germans
Po'sa taiboo	Crazy White Man	Adolf Hitler
Ekasahpana	Red Stomach High Up (Red Sashes)	Soldiers

son of the former president, was the deputy commander and led the 4th Division onto the beach. His orderly, radio operator, and driver was Larry Saupitty, a Comanche code talker. Saupitty was the one who sent the first message from the shore. The 4th Division had landed a few thousand yards from its

Comanche Code Word/Phrase	English Translation	English Code Word or Meaning
Pohpituu ekasahpana	Jump Soldiers	Paratroopers
Natusu'u kahni	Medicine House	Hospital
Kahni	Any Dwelling	House
Wakaree'e	Turtle	Tank
Kunawaikina pu'e	Fire Wagon Road	Railroad
Navaaka utsa	Bullet Place	Ammo Dump
Ta wo'i	Any Gun	Rifle, Pistol
Ta wo'l nahuu	Gun Knife	Bayonet
Tutsahkuna tawo'i	Sewing Machine Gun	.30 Caliber Machine Gun
Ekasahpana' piatowo'i	Soldier's Big Gun	Bazooka
Piata' wo'i'	Big Gun	Artillery
Tuephuhtsatu	Small Explosion	Hand Grenade
Tutaatu piata'wo'i'	Small Big Gun	105 Howitzer
Puhtsa'etu	Goes Off By Itself	Landmine
Nakohto ta'wo'i'	Stove Gun	Mortar
Navaaka	Its Arrow	Bullets, Shells
Nauukuwaa	Without A Horse	Car
Pawovipuku	Boat	Any Boat
Piapawovipuku	Big Boat	Ship
Punnutsa yutsu'etu	Flies By Itself	Airplane
Hutsuu no'avakatu	Pregnant Bird	Bomber
Punnutsa yutsu nahr'etu	They Fight Flies By Itself	Fighter
Piavoi piapu'e	Big Road	Highway
Tunaki	Listening	Radio

* Partial list From William C. Meadows's *The Comanche Code Talkers of World War II* (Austin: University of Texas Press, 2002), 235–240.

designated area of attack and Brigadier General Roosevelt had to let the command ship know about the mistake so that the next set of troops would not assault the wrong area and suffer heavy casualties. Since Roosevelt did not want the Germans intercepting this crucial information, he had Saupitty send it in code. Because he was in the wrong place, Roosevelt had to make the decision to move inland from where he stood or double back to his designated landing zone and head inland from there. Roosevelt decided to start from where he stood. Saupitty was with Roosevelt when he gave the famous order: "This is as good a place as any to start the war. We'll start right here."[124]

The code talkers did indeed "start right here." From that point on from Utah Beach, they took part in most of the major battles leading to the end of the war in Europe. The 4th Division took part in the battle for Cherbourg in Normandy and fought the battle of the Hedgerows until Operation Cobra, the great breakout campaign through Saint-Lô. The code talkers had laid communications wire in preparation for the operation, fell back, and dug in. The Allied bombing that took place tragically fell on some U.S. troops, killing nearly a thousand of them. One code talker said that there "wasn't a living thing left out there." However, the breakthrough under General Patton's 3rd Army went forward, carrying the 4th Division in its wake.

The 4th was also involved in the operation that liberated Paris in August 1944. In the lightning-fast operations that followed the liberation of the city, the code talkers reached the German border in September. Even though the 4th Division battled at the Siegfried Line, as the German border defenses were called, it was sent into combat in Hürtgen Forest from November 7 to December 6. After the Hürtgen Forest, the 4th was sent to Luxembourg for its first stand-down since D-Day. The 4th rested only 10 days; the code talkers had no time off because they ended up on a detail tasked with fixing the land lines that had been used by another unit. On December 16, the Germans launched their Ardennes offensive that came to be known as the Battle of the Bulge. The 4th went out to meet the German attack and fought a terrible, lengthy battle that lasted until December 26. The code talkers ended the war on the Austrian border.[125]

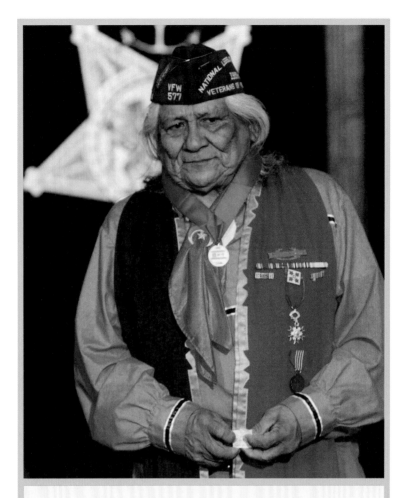

Charles Chibitty, the last surviving Comanche code talker, is pictured here on November 30, 1999, after receiving the Knowlton Award for his work in army intelligence during World War II. Chibitty passed away in July 2005 at the age of 83.

Unlike their Navajo counterparts, the contributions of the Comanche code talkers went unnoticed for 40 years. They earned their share of medals and were one of the few army units to be in almost constant action from D-Day to the end of the war. Even their hard-earned "rest" in Luxembourg was disrupted by the Battle of the Bulge. Ultimately, they did their part in helping the Allies win the war. But more than that, their great contribution to the war effort was about bringing the war to an end as quickly as possible in order to stop the further loss of life. As the late code talker Roderick Red Elk put it:

> I think it [the code] gave the Army a means of communications that they would not have otherwise had . . . some of the messages they sent might have been sent [without using the code], but they could have been . . . decoded by the Germans. Because right there at the first I think that they were in such a rush to get some of those messages through that they might have been easily intercepted. And I think the impact that the code talkers had was the fact that they had this code that they use which . . . the enemy couldn't break. That was really an advantage that the Army had. . . . It definitely saved some lives.[126]

The War at Home

THE WAR TOUCHED NEARLY EVERY NATIVE AMERICAN'S life. If they were not directly involved in the fighting, they were working in war industries, buying war bonds, and even surrendering some of their land to the war effort. The war marked an unprecedented transition in Native American life; Indian families became more mobile and Native Americans, as individuals, became more aware of their status under U.S. law.

MEDIA COVERAGE OF THE NATIVE AMERICAN WAR EFFORT

The fact that Native Americans were commited to the war effort, as reported in the media, gave all Americans a boost in their sense of democratic and liberal superiority. In this case, an entire group of people, with a few minor exceptions, had devoted itself to the American crusade despite their poverty and status as secondary citizens. At the time, nearly every non-Indian in the country would have agreed that Native Americans had benefited the least from the United

States being a great military and economic power. The whole of North America had been taken from or surrendered, as a result of armed clashes, by Native Americans. In return, these indigenous peoples had been imprisoned on tiny remnants of once vast homelands, placed in the legal position of wardship under the federal government, and left as the poorest of the nation's poor. That the great majority of Native Americans had not been impressed with Nazi propaganda

Sioux members of the U.S. armed forces show Chief White Bull of the Standing Rock Sioux a .50-caliber machine gun. Approximately 2,000 men from the Pine Ridge, Rosebud, and Standing Rock Sioux reservations served in World War II. From left to right are Corporal Ben Elk Eagle, Chief White Bull, Private William Bird Horse, Private Owen Last Horse, and Private Philip Good Buffalo.

and, in fact, stood ready to fight on the side of the United States, reassured the rest of America that, despite its history of mistreating Indians, the American system of justice would prevail and right the past wrongs done to its Native American citizens. That was the hope of most non-Indians, as well as that of most Native Americans.

For most Americans, World War II was a duel to the death between American democracy and Fascist injustice. In throwing themselves into the war effort, Native Americans validated the American sense of mission. As one Columbia River tribal member put it: "We know that under Nazism we should have no rights at all; we should be used as slaves." If oppressed peoples sided with the United States, then logically the American crusade was a just cause.

The media's opinion of Native Americans during the war years was decidedly ambiguous. Generally, the press viewed the Indian war effort as a great shot in the arm for national morale. In addition to making "chiefs" and "princesses" of many of the Allied leaders—Eleanor Roosevelt and the consort queen of England included—Native American elders and politicians, independently declared war on Germany, Italy, and Japan. Many of these same leaders posed for newspaper and magazine photographs in their own war bonnets with gray-haired politicians, as well as with young Indian men in their new, crisp uniforms. Native Americans also sang and danced for war-bond rallies. The entire press coverage of American Indians in the war was geared to give the impression that native people were not only aiding white Americans in the war, either in uniform or in the factories making weapons, but also fervently hoping to share in the victory over Fascism. Native Americans, for the time being, were no longer seen as ruthless savages standing in the way of progress, but as noble warriors standing shoulder to shoulder with the Americans in their quest to rid the world of totalitarian governments (except the Soviet Union for the time being).

The motion-picture industry was a little behind the print media in its presentation of Native Americans, but not by much. Most movies in the period continued to portray Indians as savages and barriers to westward expansion. Typically these "horse operas" glorified the imaginary American frontier fighting spirit that overcame the Native American menace to the white cowboy and pioneer. In a few Westerns, however, there appeared more and more the character of the "Indian companion" who, as in the war, aided the white, male hero in his crusade against injustice. The Red Ryder films, for example, featured a boy companion by the name of "Little Beaver." And Hawkeye's noble companions, Chingachgook and Uncas, were featured in several remakes of James Fennimore Cooper's *The Last of the Mohicans.* The Red Ryder films were directly taken from the radio programs of the same title. Radio broadcasts were, in fact, well ahead of their motion-picture contemporaries. *The Lone Ranger,* a radio staple, had the title character and his "faithful companion" Tonto combating evil on the fictional frontier well before World War II broke out.[127]

WORKING FOR VICTORY

Of course, Native Americans did much more than lend their cultures and faces, as well as the stereotypes whites had of them, to the effort to boost American morale. In addition to performing at war-bond rallies, Native Americans purchased war bonds and stamps. War bonds and stamps were just one way in which the United States financed the war and also got the public involved in the effort to defeat the Axis Powers. The idea of getting the public deeply involved in the war effort was essential. The economics of the war was almost cyclical: War industries hired those who were not fighting; the workers, in turn, purchased the bonds that replenished the U.S. Treasury with the money they earned on the job; and the money from the bonds paid for the planes, tanks, uniforms, guns, and munitions used in fighting the nation's enemies. The workers were making the tools of war and paying for them at the same time.

Very early on in the war, Native Americans were purchasing war bonds as members of their larger tribal entities

BUY WAR BONDS

In addition to their contributions in battle, Native Americans also assisted in the war effort at home. Many Native Americans purchased war bonds and donated money to the war effort. Depicted here is a poster promoting the purchase of war bonds to support the U.S. war effort.

and as individual citizens. In early 1942, for example, the Creek Nation and allied Euchee tribe bought $400,000 in war bonds. In 1943, the Wind River Shoshone Nation purchased $500 war bonds for each of its members. The Crow Nation of Montana sent $10,000 directly to President Roosevelt and pledged its entire buffalo herd to the use of the federal government in the war effort. By the end of 1942, Native American spending on war bonds amounted to $2,671,625. In 1944, Commissioner of Indian Affairs John Collier estimated that the total Native American contribution to the war effort in monetary terms amounted to some $50 million. Native Americans also contributed to the Red Cross. Some, like a group of Osage women in Oklahoma, sewed bandages; others, notably the women of Taos Pueblo in New Mexico, knitted them. The Navajos outdid most of these efforts in setting agricultural production quotas on the reservation and pledged the use of the nation's sawmill, packing plant, and flour mill to the federal government. Tribal Chairman Chee Dodge was said to have bought $20,000 worth of war bonds.[128, 129]

Throughout the war, Native American men and women who were not already in the armed forces left the reservations to find work in U.S. cities. The war had expanded industry and the U.S. economy was booming. Between 1941 and 1944, more than 40,000 American Indians, or 10 percent of their population, left their rural homes to work in the factories that produced the armaments of war. John Collier called this movement "the greatest exodus of Indians" ever to take place. (He was wrong: During the 1830s, more Native Americans were forced to move from their eastern homelands to reservations west of the Mississippi River as a result of the country's removal policies.) This movement to America's industrial centers was nevertheless viewed as an inspiring Native American commitment to the war effort.

THE GREAT LAND GIVEAWAY

On the reservations, which were running critically short of male workers by 1944, Native American women accounted for much of the food production, and even produced surpluses in some areas. Principally because of Native American women, the production of Indian livestock had doubled in the years between 1933 and 1943. Grain and farm production increased significantly, too. By 1945, it was estimated that 150,000 Native Americans directly participated in the industrial, agricultural, and military segments of the total American war effort.[130]

The reservations, which in the nineteenth century were considered nearly worthless pieces of territory, were now coveted by the federal government for numerous reasons. The government not only sought Native American mineral, oil, and lumber resources for the war effort, but also the additional space for bases, sites for bombing practice, and gunnery ranges. In South Dakota, the Lakota and Dakota peoples handed over 300,000 acres for gunnery practice. In Arizona, the Gila River Reservation and the Tohono O'odham Nation turned over a vast amount of acreage for use as bombing ranges. Ironically, the U.S. Navy even leased 50 acres of land from the Pyramid Lake Reservation in landlocked Nevada.

It was thought that surrendering these lands would have little effect on the peoples of the reservations, since they were thinly populated anyway. But after the government leased 300,000 acres of the Pine Ridge Reservation in South Dakota, a number of Oglala Lakota families were suddenly uprooted, not to be compensated for the homes, crops, land, or way of life for more than a decade. In Oklahoma, several Cherokee families were similarly dislocated when the U.S. War Department purchased 32,000 acres at Camp Gruber for a fraction of what the land was worth. Overall, the federal government leased or purchased nearly 900,000 acres of Native American land, some of which to this day has not been returned or allowed to be bought back.[131]

In one of the more disturbing moments in American history, the federal government established the War Relocation Authority, first under the direction of Milton Eisenhower and later under Dillon S. Myer, to round up and incarcerate Japanese immigrants and Japanese-American citizens. As later historians would point out, this relocation was not only unconstitutional but was also very reminiscent of the way the U.S. forced Native Americans from their homelands or compelled them to live on smaller and smaller pieces of their own territories. Once the relocation of the Japanese Americans began, Commissioner John Collier proposed that Eisenhower use Indian lands as sites for the internment camps. Collier argued that Indian lands were perfect locations for these camps because they were inland, away from the primary war factories on the West Coast, and were sparsely populated. He also wanted to add to the idea that Native Americans were just as committed to the war as any other American group.

Ultimately, three locations on Native American lands were selected for the internment campsites. The first was the Colorado River Reservation on the Arizona side of the Arizona-California border. According to Collier, the reservation had at least 10,000 acres available because there were only 1,300 Mohave and Chemehuevi people—some of whom had already entered the military or were working in the war industry factories—living there. The second was on the Gila River Reservation near Phoenix, Arizona. This reservation was the home of the Pima and Maricopa peoples. The third camp was to be located on the Leupp Indian Plant (named for former commissioner of Indian Affairs Francis E. Leupp) in Winslow, Arizona.

THE QUESTION OF INDIAN SOVEREIGNTY ARISES ONCE AGAIN

Some Native Americans protested against placing the Japanese Americans on Indian lands. Several residents of the Colorado River Reservation opposed the idea and recorded their objections to their Indian Office superintendent, Charles Gensler. In turn, Gensler argued that creating an internment camp would hinder agricultural production because it would tie up a large amount of land in providing living space for the Japanese Americans. Additionally, both the Navajos and the Pimas and Maricopas were leery of having the evacuees located near their own homes. The propaganda of the time portrayed the Japanese as particularly evil enemies. But under the 1934 Indian Reorganization Act, Commissioner Collier had the power to lease the property of those tribes that came under federal legal jurisdiction without consultation or higher authority. His arbitrary use of that power raised another, more important question that ranked above simply placing the 25,000 interned Japanese Americans on Indian lands. If he could lease Indian lands without consultation or higher authority, then were Native American nations truly sovereign? It certainly appeared that Collier usurped power by placing these internment camps on Native American land. This question would be raised once again following the war when Congress decided to terminate the federal government's trust responsibility to Native American nations.[132, 133]

Native Americans generously sacrificed for the war effort; not only their money, minerals, and land but also their labor and, in many cases, their age-old customs and practices. It was one of the greatest periods of cultural transition in Native American history. But sacrifices would unfortunately be misinterpreted and the federal government would attempt to use the memory of those sacrifices to bring about a sudden, unexpected, and disastrous change in Indian policy.

The Legacy of Native American Participation in World War II

DURING WORLD WAR II, NATIVE AMERICANS HAD FLUNG themselves into the war effort. Their record of valor in combat, hard work in the war industries, and generosity in giving what little they had in terms of manpower, land, and treasure toward winning the war was without equal given their relative population. Indeed, their participation in World War II was so extensive that it would become a part of American folklore and popular culture. It was a magnificent gesture worthy of a great people, yet it was also one that would provide little consolation.

TERMINATING THE TRUST RESPONSIBILITY

Even before the war's end, the notion of fully assimilating Native Americans into mainstream American society was retooled from being a simple landgrab to an elaborate, liberal-sounding plan to "amalgamate" Indians by doing away with the United States' trust relationship with Indian nations and turning reservation lands into private property. Prior to the war, the agitation in favor of ending the treaty-bound trust responsibilities of the United States with Indian nations was a conservative effort to undo President Franklin D. Roosevelt's New Deal and reduce the size of government. Because of the overwhelming Native American commitment to the U.S. war effort, however, the anti-Roosevelt conservative forces began to couch their insistence on dropping the trust relationship in liberal terms.

In 1944, Oswald Garrison Villard, writing for *Christian Century*, reaffirmed the Native American contribution to the war effort and assured readers that the thousands of Indians fighting overseas and working in war industries were in actuality striving to become part of the American mainstream. "Their sole request is that they are awarded citizenship like other Americans," he wrote, "a citizenship unhampered by restrictions which do not apply to everybody." Reservations and federal guardianship, according to Villard, were oppressive and sounded like the totalitarian states Americans were fighting against. He was convinced that most Native American men and women no longer wanted "to stay at home and be confined within the reservations."

Although Villard sought "to break up no reservation," his argument was directed toward that very goal. In his view, tribal cultures, arts, and ceremonies were unique and worthy of being recorded but equally doomed to extinction. Native Americans would tire, according to Villard, "of being considered circus exhibits." Allowing the Native American to continue to live according to custom would mean "halting his modern adaptation." Standing in the way of getting Indians off the reservations was the Indian Bureau, which Villard wanted liquidated.[134]

Writer O. K. Armstrong made the strongest statement in favor of "amalgamation" in a 1945 article for the popular magazine *Reader's Digest.* Armstrong claimed to have interviewed Native Americans from around the country and found them with an "unmistakable determination" to "demand full rights of citizenship." Armstrong was certain that younger Indians were going to lead a movement that would eventually "set their people free" from the entanglements of government bureaucracy. Indian veterans, he said, "who return from the service will seek a greater share in American freedom." The others who had labored in the factories and had "tasted economic opportunity for the first time" would not be satisfied, as Armstrong put it, "to live in a shack and loaf around in a blanket."

Armstrong saved his heaviest ammunition for an attack on the Bureau of Indian Affairs. In the 12 years since John

As World War II came to a close in 1945, writer O. K. Armstrong promoted the idea that Native Americans were in favor of banding together to demand full rights as American citizens. Armstrong largely blamed the head of the Bureau of Indian Affairs, John Collier (pictured here standing with a group of Flatheads in 1935), for attempting to regiment Native Americans by promoting the reservation system.

Collier had been its commissioner, Indian policy and the bureau itself had undergone great change. Since the passage of the Indian Reorganization Act (IRA) in 1934, tribes could form governments, the allotment of Indian lands had ceased, a loan system had been set up to aid the establishment of tribal businesses, and, in general, the policy of trying to destroy Native American cultures had been curbed. In Armstrong's view, the IRA marked a return to the nineteenth-century goal of Indian assimilation. According to Armstrong, the IRA had forced "a collectivist system upon the Indians, with bigger doses of paternalism and regimentation." Under it, bureaucracy had grown out of control and had placed an even greater burden on the American taxpayer. After attacking Collier's bureau in conservative terms—he very nearly called Collier a communist—Armstrong went on to put a liberal spin on his message. The whole Collier policy, in Armstrong's eyes, was not aimed at protecting Indian lands but maintaining the reservations as a method of "racial segregation."[135]

Villard's and Armstrong's ideas represented a striking paradox in American thought. Their notions were well within the boundaries of both conservative and liberal traditions. They were certainly conservative in that they advocated a policy of less government regulation. At the same time, they argued that the reservation system was a policy based on segregating a particular people due to their race. In their minds, freeing "the Indian" meant not protecting tribally owned property, but rather desegregating American society. Incidentally, the federal government would free itself of long-held legal responsibilities.

Following the publication of Armstrong's article, the *American Indian Magazine,* which was the editorial arm of the American Association on Indian Affairs, printed a series of rebuttals to these ideas. Haven Emerson, the president of the organization, wrote that Armstrong's article was "an ill-informed rehash of old fallacies and sentiments" and a "potential danger to the very freedoms which it demands." Emerson was of the opinion that Armstrong sounded a great deal like the people who, in the previous century, had advocated the policy of allotting Indian lands and selling off the surplus to land speculation companies—a policy that proved itself to be a disastrous mistake. Rather than being an "outdoor prison," a reservation was a homeland that could be developed to benefit Native Americans economically. Indians were already U.S. citizens and could leave their reservations if they so desired. But the foundation of Native American liberty and future development was the tribal land base. And protecting that land base was the U.S. government's first priority.

Views such as Villard's and Armstrong's, however, were far more compelling to white Americans fresh from the struggle against Nazi tyranny and on the verge of launching another crusade against Communism. Native Americans had fought for freedom shoulder to shoulder with the white man, yet had been forced to return to the grinding poverty of the reservations. They were, according to writers like Villard and Armstrong, being segregated from the very society they had helped protect against Axis aggression. The government was supporting what they believed was a restrictive and oppressive system with their taxes. Although these arguments were grossly fallacious, they provided the moral rhetoric needed to dismantle Roosevelt's New Deal, especially the Bureau of Indian Affairs.

The process of "freeing" Native Americans (from their land) and coincidentally relieving the federal government of its responsibilities began immediately following World War II. In 1946, Congress created the Indian Claims Commission in order to adjudicate various clams made by native peoples against the United States. In large part the establishment of the commission was an attempt to do justice to those Indians who had suffered at the hands of the federal government. On the other hand, the commission was designed to take care of suits to clear the way for an eventual withdrawal of the government from the "Indian business."

A year later, lawmakers established the Commission on the Organization of the Executive Brand of Government and appointed as its head former president Herbert Hoover. Within this commission's jurisdiction, Hoover set up an "Indian Task Force" to investigate and make recommendations on American Indian policy. In 1948, less than a year after its formation, the Hoover commission issued a bland analysis of then-current programs directed by the Bureau of Indian Affairs. Although it condemned the policy of breaking up the reservations into individually held plots of land and urged caution in making rapid changes in policy, it nevertheless insisted that "assimilation must be the dominant goal of public policy."

Nothing, it seemed, could alter the course that American Indian policy took in the 10 years following World War II. Despite protests from the newly organized National Congress of American Indians (1944) and objections from a few government officials, the U.S. government moved inexorably toward a policy of terminating the federal trust relationship with the tribes. Using the argument that the federal government was merely trying to grant the rights and freedoms of citizenship that American Indians had fought so hard for in the war, Congress reduced appropriation to the Bureau of Indian Affairs, urged the agency to promote assimilation programs such as relocating Native Americans from reservations to cities, and pressed for the complete abolishment of the protectorate status that Native American nations had negotiated for in their treaties. In 1953, Congress passed House Concurrent Resolution 108, which provided the power to terminate relations with individual Native American nations. Public Law 280 followed shortly thereafter. It actually terminated specific tribes as political entities.[136]

POPULAR IMAGES OF NATIVE AMERICANS FOLLOWING THE WAR

The policies of terminating the trust responsibility and re-locating thousands of Native Americans to urban areas resulted from incorrect but nevertheless logical—from the U.S. perspective—assumptions. During the war, large numbers of Native Americans had indeed left their reservations to join the military or to labor in factories. After Dillon Myer (the same person who headed the office that oversaw the relocation of Japanese Americans) became the new commissioner of the Bureau of Indian Affairs in 1951, he began a program that would aid the migration of more Indians to industrialized urban areas. The program provided some funds for relocating families and found jobs for the heads of these families. The unfortunate aspect of the whole project was that the relocation bureaucracy only followed up on the lives of these families for six months. Consequently, no one knows if the program was successful in the long run. During the 1950s, relocation only served to create a new Native American urban underclass, because the jobs the bureau procured for them were low-paying at best.[137]

In essence, the outpouring of support for the war effort on the part of Native Americans created the image of their people desperately seeking to overcome the poverty and isolation of the reservations. Writers like Armstrong and Villard played on the image of the Indian warrior who fought for the country but was prevented from collecting his reward by a system that segregated him on the reservation. War movies of the 1950s and 1960s, unlike Westerns, treated Indian characters much more sympathetically, but still portrayed Indians as willingly and even heroically fighting alongside the white man for a better world.

The 1961 movie *The Outsider* was the first Hollywood film that focused on the Native American war effort during World War II. In the film, Tony Curtis (right) portrays Ira Hayes, who, in the movie, is rejected by his people when he returns home after the war.

The first time the Navajo code talkers were acknowledged in film was in 1954's *Battle Cry,* starring Van Heflan, Aldo Ray, and then teen heartthrob Tab Hunter. In one scene, two Navajo code talkers are featured sending a message. These two, privates "Crazy Horse" and "Lighttower," were played by actors Felix Noriego and Jonas Applegate, respectively, and only appeared on-screen briefly. The next year, Noriego had a larger role in the film *To Hell and Back.* This movie was a chronology of Audie Murphy's service with the 3rd "Marne" Infantry Division. Murphy was the most-decorated service-man in World War II, winning the Medal of Honor and numerous other prestigious awards. Noriego played Swope, a Native American soldier and one of Murphy's platoon buddies who was eventually wounded and sent home.

In 1961, Hollywood produced *The Outsider,* which was perhaps the first film to focus on a World War II Native American serviceman. In this case, Ira H. Hayes, the Pima marine who helped raise the American flag on Mount Suribachi on Iwo Jima, was the central character and was played by another leading man, Tony Curtis. It was certainly not the first time a white man played an Indian on film, but it was a marked departure from *Battle Cry* and *To Hell and Back,* both of which actually used Native American actors.

The Outsider was Hollywood's attempt to demonstrate how America exploits heroes for a short time before casting them aside in favor of new heroes and celebrities. It was, in its way, an admirable effort and Curtis's acting showed that he was a solid character actor rather than simply a leading-man type. On the other hand, the film depicted Hayes as a rejected hero even on his home reservation, and that the effort Hayes made to fit in was all for nothing. His status as an "outsider," unable to adjust to his own as well as the white man's postwar culture, led him to alcoholism and an early death.

At the time *The Outsider* was released, very little was known about Post Traumatic Stress Disorder, or PTSD. Hayes had participated in two of the bloodiest and most horrifying battles of the war in the Pacific, Bougainville and Iwo Jima. The trauma of combat on this scale is linked to what is known as "survivors' guilt" or "age acceleration." Essentially, both emotional problems stem from seeing the deaths of people from one's own age group and dealing with the grief and the feelings that one has experienced. The symptoms of PTSD are bouts of severe depression and withdrawal from society, nightmares or sleep intrusions, heightened startle responses, feelings of intense rage that may be construed as paranoia, and realistic flashbacks triggered by various sights, smells, and sounds.

The problems associated with PTSD often bring on substance abuse. It can reasonably be assumed that Hayes suffered intensely from PTSD and became, as a result, an alcoholic. Far from being rejected by his home community, Hayes was suffering through the throes of a grave emotional problem linked to his horrific experiences in combat. He lost a tribal election to be sure, but that was quite simply the result of tribal politics rather than a rejection of Hayes. After his death, Hayes's people have honored his memory. His name is attached to a school on his home reservation, as well as a beautiful park in Sacaton, Arizona.

A number of other commercial films have, in some way or another, dealt with Native American participation in

The 2002 movie *Windtalkers* depicts the Navajo code talkers during the U.S. Marines' invasion of Saipan in June 1944. In the movie, Adam Beach (pictured here, left) and Roger Willie played the code talkers, while Nicolas Cage (pictured here, right) and Christian Slater played their bodyguards.

World War II. One of the most degrading was 1967's *The Dirty Dozen.* In it, an army major creates a suicide squad of military prisoners who have committed the crimes of rape, murder, or both. The unit attacks a villa in France that serves as a vacation spot for high-ranking German officers and their friends. The "dirty dozen" traps the villa's guests in a cellar, pours gasoline on them, and drops grenades down several airshafts to kill the entire assemblage, soldier and civilian alike. A member of the "dirty dozen" is supposed to be an Apache named Sampson Posey. Clint Walker, a white actor and star of television Westerns, played Posey with inarticulate, stereotypical stoicism.

It was not until 2002's *Windtalkers* that Hollywood produced an attempt to accurately depict a real Native American contribution to the American victory in World War II. *Windtalkers* focused on two Navajo code talkers and their "bodyguards" during the U.S. Marine invasion of Saipan. Adam Beach and Roger Willie played the code talkers, and Nicolas Cage and Christian Slater the bodyguards. For a more dramatic storyline, the writers rejuvenated the rumor that the code talker bodyguards had the specific duty of killing the individual code talker should he fall into the hands of the enemy. To that end, both Roger Willie's and Christian Slater's characters met their doom. Nicolas Cage's character, on the other hand, has the opportunity to execute the code talker played by Adam Beach but instead launches a heroic and bloody fight to save him.

CULTURAL PRESERVATION

The notion that Native American veterans would rapidly give up their culture was put to rest when they came home to participate in their communities' politics, religious rituals, and social systems. A remarkable number of warrior societies and their dances were rejuvenated. The Pawnees, Otoes,

(continues on page 144)

THE REVIVAL OF THE KIOWA GOURD DANCE

The Gourd Dance is the ceremony of a traditional Kiowa warrior society. Known as the *Tia-piah,* the society served as a police force during the annual Sun Dance and the great summer buffalo hunts. In fact, the Gourd Dance usually preceded the erection of the Sun Dance lodge and more or less set the boundaries for the preeminent Kiowa religious ceremony.

There are numerous stories regarding how the Tia-piah got its start, but the most prevalent is the story of the Red Wolf and the lone Kiowa warrior. It seems that this particular warrior had been separated from the rest of his hunting party and was heading for his village on his own. As he was traveling, he happened to hear a melodious voice in the distance. He turned his horse and moved toward the unknown singer. As he reached the top of a rise on the prairie landscape, he caught sight of a great Red Wolf with its paw on a shiny object. The wolf was shaking a rattle made of a wooden shaft and a silver shaker. The Red Wolf was singing the most beautiful song the warrior had ever heard.

The warrior sat on the prairie all night long, transfixed by the beautiful songs. His spirit was uplifted and he could hardly stop moving in time with Red Wolf's gourd. Finally Red Wolf spoke to the warrior: "I am giving you these songs and this new dance for you to take back to your people. The Kiowas will keep these songs and this dance." When the warrior returned home, he told this story to the Kiowa people and they started celebrating the gifts Red Wolf had presented to the lone warrior. To this day, Gourd Dance singers and dancers end the songs with a wolf howl, a shake of the gourd, and a drum roll to show their appreciation to Red Wolf.

The Kiowa chiefs formed the Gourd Dance Society (or Clan) as a warriors' group to carry on Red Wolf's gift and to defend and

(continues)

(continued)

police the Kiowa villages. These warriors fought a great battle on a place that was covered with skunkberry bushes. The bushes were in full bloom with their red berries. The color red was everywhere and the blood from the battle made the landscape seem as if a crimson blanket had covered the prairie. Today the ceremony dancers drape their shoulders with a Gourd Dance blanket, the red portion of which symbolizes this great battle.

Kiowa sacred history contains many stories about the Gourd Dance and the three sacred objects—the rope, the whip, and the bugle—that have become symbols of the society's courage in battle and the persistence of Kiowa knowledge, ethics, and culture. Even so, the society nearly met its demise in the early twentieth century. New religions—Christianity and the Native American Church—had come to the Kiowas in the last half of the nineteenth century. The missionaries who had come to the Kiowa people as agents of the federal government continually urged them to give up their Sun Dance, the principal Kiowa annual ceremonial that renewed the people's relationship with the spirit world. The missionaries also exhorted them to get rid of their warrior ways, which meant, of course, the end of the war ceremonies and the warrior societies. All this led to the deterioration of the traditional Kiowa rituals, including the Sun Dance. Since the Gourd Dance was usually held around the same time as the Sun Dance, the two had been closely associated. Thus, when the Kiowas gave up the Sun Dance, they continued to attend the Gourd Dance as a kind of ceremonial substitute to several Kiowa rituals. Both ceremonies were held during the summer and the Gourd Dance became an annual event held on July 4. Since the United States was celebrating its independence, this was the only time the Kiowas had a break in work that corresponded to the time when the ceremony was traditionally held.

The Gourd Dance was held sporadically during the period between 1890 and 1917. The U.S. Bureau of Indian Affairs officially frowned upon any form of Native American dancing, especially those that continued the "martial spirit" among the tribes. When Native American soldiers and sailors returned from World War I, several tribes attempted to revive those ceremonies linked to honoring or purifying warriors following a conflict. Many of the Indian agents, by and large acting on their own authority, worked hard to prevent these ceremonies and, unfortunately for some, their labors ended in the abandonment of these time-honored rituals. The Kiowa Gourd Dance, while it was not forgotten, fell into disuse.

World War II brought on an effort to revitalize the Gourd Dance. In 1941, Bill Koomsa Sr., and several others began to practice a series of Gourd Dance songs with an eye toward reviving the ceremony. A Gourd Dance was held in 1943 at the city park in Carnegie, Oklahoma, but the society and the ceremony itself did not get started in earnest until Kiowa veterans began to return home from the battlefields of World War II. Although they joined veterans' organizations, the Kiowas generally felt that groups like the American Legion and the Veterans of Foreign War (VFW) did not meet Native American needs. A number of distinctly native cultural activities seemed to help restore the community relations that the veterans had missed during their tours of duty, because they were primarily fighting alongside non-Indians. War Mothers' Society dances were held; powwows with "war dances" became more frequent in the relatively better financial times following the war; and warrior societies, including the Kiowa Gourd Clan, were revived for good.

The Kiowa Gourd Clan began its annual ceremonies following World War II. Since then, it has split into at least two main groups. The first retains the name Kiowa Gourd Clan and is a society exclusive to Kiowas. Other people, noting that as far back as 1916 members of the Otoes had been included in the ceremonies, formed a splinter group that became known as Tia-piah. That group opened

(continues)

(continued)

its membership to those who have demonstrated good character and maintained the values the Gourd Dance represents: respect for tradition, morality, courage, sacrifice, and honor.

Today, the Gourd Dance usually leads off a southern-style powwow and involves a number of people, usually veterans, from all tribes. Since its revival and the intertribal nature of modern powwows, the Gourd Dance has been adopted by many tribes. The participants usually are requested to dress appropriately. Most have adopted the red and blue blanket draped over their shoulders, the bandolier made of silver beads and mescal beans, and a sash. Military decorations and beaded medallions adorn their blankets. The dancers shake rattles made of metal (tin salt and pepper shakers are acceptable) or real dried gourds with beaded or decorated handles, and they hold fans of eagle, hawk, or macaw feathers. Most of the Kiowa elders say that dress pants, white shirts, and even men's ties are appropriate dress for the Gourd Dance. Mostly, though, modern Gourd Dancers wear long-sleeved shirts, "street" shoes or cowboy boots, and some type of trousers other than blue jeans. Short-sleeve shirts and T-shirts are frowned upon. Several Gourd Dance societies have now created their own logos and wear them on specially made vests in place of the red and blue blankets.

(continued from page 140)

Osages, Poncas, and others in Oklahoma began to hold *heyluska* dances on a regular basis. The Omaha people of Nebraska had already held these men's dances and their revival was essential to the continuance of these tribes as distinct groups. The Cheyennes revived their Bowstring society and the Crazy Dog dances. The Kiowa Gourd Dance, originally a warrior society ceremony, became a truly intertribal veterans' ritual. Navajos came home to ceremonies that had been arranged by their families to purify their spirits and pave the way for their reentry into Navajo society. Cherokee veterans took part in ceremonies designed to cleanse them of the trauma of battle and to "wash the blood from their hands" in order to take part in tribal religious ceremonies. Many veterans who were members of the Native American Church held special peyote ceremonies. Veterans ran for and won seats on tribal councils and became tribal chairpersons. All in all, Native American veterans were adamant about preserving their heritage and maintaining their status as members of their nations.

In many ways, the legacy of Native American participation in World War II is troubling. Service in the military always seems to be interpreted as either an attempt to legitimize citizenship or an agreement with a given nation's political will. Native American service in the military and in war industries was for many years explained as the overriding endeavor of Native Americans to enter mainstream American society. The remaining Indian lands were viewed as unwanted and unproductive. Given that these views were presented by the media, there can be little wonder why the federal government proceeded with the termination and relocation policies. Additionally, hardly anyone knew of the emotional problems that plagued Native American combat veterans. Moreover, white policy makers and writers did not know at the time that age-old tribal ceremonies held the key to curing these diseases of the mind and spirit. The white "experts" of the period wrote off what became known as PTSD as a symptom of poverty and of being segregated from the American mainstream. The tribal cultures that produced these ceremonies of healing, purification, and reentry into society were said to be archaic and "backward" remnants of ways of life that no longer had relevance to those people wanting to enter the larger society. It has taken nearly 60 years and a great deal of study to present a more accurate and critical look at the consequences of Native American service in the war effort of 1941 to 1945.

Chronology

1940 *JUNE*   The Navajo Nation issues a proclamation pledging unwavering support for the United States should it go to war.

SEPTEMBER   Congress passes the Selective Training and Service Act; some Native people protest being drafted, but most gladly sign up.

DECEMBER   The U.S. Army begins recruiting Comanche code talkers.

1941 *MARCH*   Congress passes the Lend-Lease Act, and soon U.S. ships are engaged in the Battle of the Atlantic against German submarine "wolf packs."

DECEMBER   Japan attacks Hawaii, the Philippines, Singapore, and several other Dutch, British, and American-held islands in the Pacific; the United States declares war on Japan; Germany declares war on the United States; the land battle for the Philippines begins.

1942 *JANUARY*   Jemez Pueblo declares war on the Axis Powers (Germany, Japan, and Italy).

MARCH   The Battle for New Guinea begins with Australian troops bearing the brunt of the fighting against the Japanese.

APRIL   Bataan in the Philippines falls; the Bataan Death March begins; the first group of Navajo code talkers is recruited.

MAY   Battle of the Coral Sea; the bombing campaign from Great Britain begins; the thousand plane bombing raid on Cologne, Germany, takes place; U.S. bombers begin arriving in Great Britain.

JUNE   Battle of Midway Island; Osage general Clarence Tinker dies in a bomber crash en route to Hawaii from the Midway battle; the Iroquois Confederacy, and the Ponca, Osage, Dakota, and Michigan Chippewa nations declare war on the Axis Powers.

AUGUST   Operation Watchtower; U.S. Marines land on Guadalcanal; the Navajo code talkers experience their first taste of combat.

SEPTEMBER   The U.S. 32nd Division lands in New Guinea to reinforce Australian and U.S. troops there fighting the Japanese; the arduous New Guinea campaign begins.

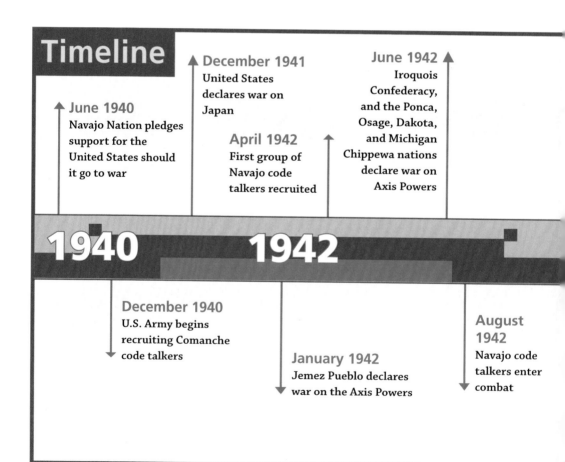

Timeline

December 1941
United States declares war on Japan

June 1942
Iroquois Confederacy, and the Ponca, Osage, Dakota, and Michigan Chippewa nations declare war on Axis Powers

June 1940
Navajo Nation pledges support for the United States should it go to war

April 1942
First group of Navajo code talkers recruited

1940   **1942**

December 1940
U.S. Army begins recruiting Comanche code talkers

January 1942
Jemez Pueblo declares war on the Axis Powers

August 1942
Navajo code talkers enter combat

NOVEMBER Operation Torch; U.S. troops land in North Africa.

1943 *JANUARY* Casablanca Conference; Roosevelt and Churchill agree to invade Sicily and Italy and combine the British and U.S. bombing campaigns over western Europe; the British bomb at night, the Americans during the day.

MARCH U.S. troop buildup in New Guinea.

JULY Operation Husky; U.S. troops land in Sicily.

SEPTEMBER Italy surrenders; the Italian campaign begins; U.S. troops land at Salerno,

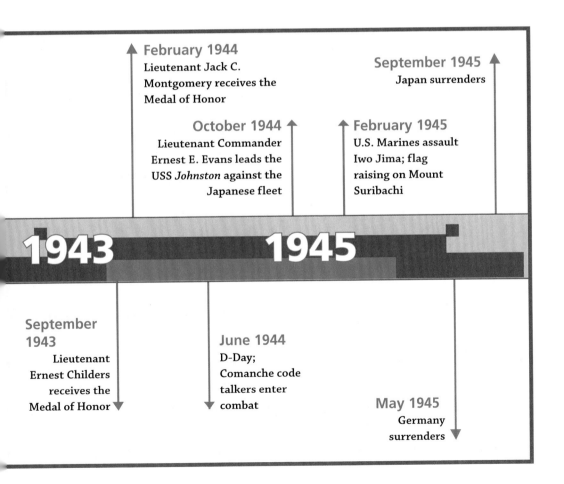

February 1944
Lieutenant Jack C. Montgomery receives the Medal of Honor

September 1945
Japan surrenders

October 1944
Lieutenant Commander Ernest E. Evans leads the USS *Johnston* against the Japanese fleet

February 1945
U.S. Marines assault Iwo Jima; flag raising on Mount Suribachi

1943

1945

September 1943
Lieutenant Ernest Childers receives the Medal of Honor

June 1944
D-Day; Comanche code talkers enter combat

May 1945
Germany surrenders

Italy; General MacArthur initiates Operation Cartwheel in the Pacific; Lieutenant Ernest Childers's actions in Italy lead to him receiving the Congressional Medal of Honor.

NOVEMBER U.S. troops land in Bougainville; the Central Pacific campaign begins; Tarawa and Makin islands attacked.

1944 *FEBRUARY* U.S. Marines attack Kwajalein and Eniwetok islands; more U.S. landings in New Guinea; U.S. troops land at Anzio, Italy; Lieutenant Jack C. Montgomery's actions in the Italian campaign lead to him receiving the Congressional Medal of Honor.

JUNE D-Day; Allied troops land in Normandy, France; the Comanche code talkers experience their first taste of combat; the Soviet Union launches Operation Bagration against Germany; in the Pacific, U.S. Marines land on Saipan; the Great Marianas Turkey Shoot takes place in the Philippine Sea.

JULY U.S. Army and Marine troops invade Guam and Tinian in the Pacific; Operation Cobra begins in France; Americans of the 3rd Army break out of Normandy and dash toward Germany.

AUGUST Operation Anvil/Dragoon; the Americans invade southern France; liberation of Paris.

SEPTEMBER Marines land on Peleliu in the Palaus; Allied forces from Normandy and southern France link near Dijon, France.

OCTOBER U.S. forces attack the Siegfried Line; U.S. Army forces land in Leyte Gulf; the sea Battle of Leyte Gulf begins; Lieutenant Commander Ernest E. Evans, captain of the USS *Johnston,* leads his ship in a suicidal attack on the Japanese fleet; his actions lead to his posthumous award of the Congressional Medal of Honor.

DECEMBER Battle of the Bulge; Bastogne relieved.

1945 *FEBRUARY* Yalta Conference; the Allies reach the Rhine River; U.S. Marines assault Iwo Jima; flag raising on Mount Suribachi; U.S. B-29s bomb Tokyo, Japan.

MARCH Siegfried Line breached; U.S. Army forces cross the Rhine at Remagen; Corregidor and Manila, capital of the Philippines, fall to the U.S. armed forces; mass incendiary bombing raid on Tokyo; U.S. troops land on Cebu Island.

APRIL U.S. forces assault Okinawa; heavy kamikaze suicide strikes against the fleet surrounding Okinawa; President Roosevelt dies of a heart attack; Soviet troops take Berlin; Adolf Hitler commits suicide.

MAY Germany surrenders.

JUNE All of the Philippines are considered secured.

JULY Potsdam Conference; President Truman hints to Stalin that the United States has the atomic bomb; the Soviet Union agrees to enter the war against Japan.

AUGUST Atomic bombs dropped on Hiroshima and Nagasaki, Japan; the Soviet Union attacks the Japanese in Manchuria; Japan accepts terms of surrender.

SEPTEMBER Japanese officials sign the instrument of surrender on the USS *Missouri* under the direction of General Douglas MacArthur.

Notes

Chapter 1

1. Ross Hassig, *Aztec Warfare: Imperial Expansion and Political Control* (Norman: University of Oklahoma Press, 1995), 236–267.
2. Patrick M. Malone, *The Skulking Way of War: Technology and Tactics Among the New England Indians* (Baltimore: The Johns Hopkins University Press, 1993), 102–105.
3. Armstrong Starkey, *European and Native American Warfare, 1675–1815* (Norman: University of Oklahoma Press, 1998).
4. Gregory Evans Dowd, *A Spirited Resistance: The North American Indian Struggle for Unity, 1745–1815* (Baltimore: The Johns Hopkins University Press, 1993).
5. James Smith, *An Account of the Remarkable Occurrences in the Life and Travels of Col. James Smith During His Captivity with the Indians in the Years 1755, '56, '57, '58, & '59.* Reprinted in Archibald Loudon. 1808 and 1811. *A Selection of Some of the Most Interesting Narratives of Outrages Committed by the Indians in Their Wars with the White People,* 2 vols. First reprint Harrisburg: Harrisburg Publishing Company, 1888. Second reprint New York: Arno Press, 1971, 241–251.
6. Thomas W. Dunlay, *Wolves for the Blue Soldiers: Indian Scouts and Auxiliaries with the United States Army, 1860–90* (Lincoln: University of Nebraska Press, 1987), 14.
7. Colin G. Calloway, *The American Revolution in Indian Country: Crisis and Diversity in Native American Communities* (New York: Cambridge University Press, 1995).
8. Fred Gearing, *Priests and Warriors: Social Structures for Cherokee Politics in the 18th Century* (Menasha, Wisc. American Anthropological Association, 1962).
9. Tom Holm, "American Indian Warfare: The Cycles of Conflict and the Militarization of Native North America," in *A Companion to American Indian History,* Philip J. Deloria and Neal Salisbury, eds. (Malden, Mass.: Blackwell Publishing, 2002), 168–169.
10. Dowd, 106–109.
11. Wiley Sword, *President Washington's Indian War: The Struggle for the Old Northwest, 1790–1795* (Norman: University of Oklahoma Press, 1993).
12. Robert V. Remini, *Andrew Jackson and His Indian Wars* (New York: Viking, 2001), 62–69.
13. Dunlay, 11–24.

14. Annie Heloise Abel, *The American Indian in the Civil War, 1862–1865* (Lincoln: University of Nebraska Press, 1992).

15. George Washington Grayson, *A Creek Warrior for the Confederacy: The Autobiography of Chief G. W. Grayson*, ed. W. David Baird (Norman: University of Oklahoma Press, 1988).

16. Frank Cunningham, *General Stand Watie's Confederate Indians* (Norman: University of Oklahoma Press, 1998).

17. David Woodbury, "From Tahlequah to Boggy Depot: Stand Watie's Civil War," *Civil War: Magazine of the Civil War Society* 10 (September/ October 1992), 38–46.

18. Ted Alexander, "Death Song at the Crater: The Chippewa Sharpshooters of Company K," *Civil War: Magazine of the Civil War Society* 10 (September/October 1992), 24–26.

19. Lawrence Hauptman, "War Eagle of the Tuscaroras," *Civil War: Magazine of the Civil War Society* 10 (September/ October 1992), 16–17, 27–30.

20. David Woodbury, "Hasanoanda of the Tonawanda Senecas, An Iroquois at Appomattox Ely S. Parker," *Civil War: Magazine of the Civil War Society* 10 (September/October 1992), 18–23.

21. Dunlay, *Wolves for the Blue Soldiers.*

22. Tom Holm, *Strong Hearts, Wounded Souls: Native American Veterans of the Vietnam War* (Austin: University of Texas Press, 1996), 94–95.

23. Cynthia H. Enloe, *Ethnic Soldiers: State Security in Divided Societies* (New York: Penguin Books, 1980), 192–193.

24. Holm, *Strong Hearts,* 96–98.

25. Jack D. Foner, *The United States Soldier Between Two Wars, 1865–1898* (New York: Humanities Press, 1970).

26. Thomas Britten, *American Indians in World War I* (Albuquerque: University of New Mexico Press, 1997).

Chapter 2

27. Jeré Bishop Franco, *Crossing the Pond: The Native American Effort in World War II* (Denton: University of North Texas Press, 1999), 41.

28. Tom Holm, "Fighting a White Man's War: The Extent and Legacy of American Indian Participation in World War II," in *The Plains Indians of the Twentieth Century,* Peter Iverson, ed., 149–166 (Norman: University of Oklahoma Press, 1985), 150.

29. Alison R. Bernstein, *American Indians and World War II* (Norman: University of Oklahoma Press, 1991), 22–23.

30. Franco, 44.

31. Holm, "Fighting a White Man's War," 153.

32. Ibid., 152, 160.

33. Kenneth William Townsend, *World War II and the American Indian* (Albuquerque: University of

New Mexico Press, 2000), 61–62.

34. Holm, "Fighting a White Man's War," 152–152.

35. Judith Bellafaire, "Native American Women Veterans," Women in Military Service for America. Available online at *http://www.womensmemorial. org/Education/NAHM.html* (accessed December 16, 2006).

36. Franco, 79.

37. Townsend, 126–127.

38. Franco, 67.

39. Ibid., 64.

40. Townsend, 127.

41. Holm, "Fighting a White Man's War," 157.

42. Franco, 151.

43. Townsend, 81–102.

Chapter 3

44. John Keegan, *The Second World War* (New York: Penguin Books, 1990), 240–256.

45. James F. Dunnigan and Albert A. Nofi, *Victory at Sea: World War II in the Pacific* (New York: William Morrow and Company, 1995), 7–12.

46. Keegan, 258–265.

47. Ibid., 265–267.

48. Dunnigan and Nofi, 15–17, 474–475.

49. Broderick H. Johnson, ed., *Navajos and World War II* (Tsaile, Ariz.: Navajo Community College Press, 1977), 18.

50. Ibid., 11–44.

51. U.S. Department of the Interior, Office of Indian Affairs, *Indians in the War* (Chicago: Haskell Printing Department, 1945), 50–51.

52. Ibid., 14–15.

53. Townsend, 132–133.

54. Keegan, 268–278.

55. Townsend, 128.

56. Elizabeth-Anne Wheal and Stephen Pope, *The Macmillan Dictionary of the Second World War* (London: Macmillan, 1997), 200–201.

57. James Jones, *WWII: A Chronicle of Soldiering* (New York: Ballantine Books, 1975), 48–52.

58. Dunnigan and Nofi, 34–37.

59. Doris A. Paul, *The Navajo Code Talkers* (Philadelphia: Dorrance & Company, 1973), 52–53.

60. Ibid., 39.

61. Dunnigan and Nofi, 39–40.

62. Keegan, 297–307.

63. Dunnigan and Nofi, 52–55.

64. Wheal and Pope, 277–279.

65. C. Brian Kelly, *Best True Stories from World War II* (New York: Barnes and Noble, 1998), 303–304.

66. U.S. Army, "Medal of Honor Citations." Available online at *www.army.mil/cmh-pg/Moh1. htm* (accessed December 16, 2006).

67. Dunnigan and Nofi, 63–64.

68. Jones, 105–107.

69. Dunnigan and Nofi, 65.

70. "Joseph J. Clark," Available online at *www. arlingtoncemetary.net/jjclark. htm*

71. Dunnigan and Nofi, 47–50.

72. Wheal and Pope, 187–188, 202, 354, 415, 464.

73. Jones, 219.

74. Paul, 70.

75. Dunnigan and Nofi, 582.

76. Wheal and Pope, 241.

77. Bernstein, 49.
78. U.S. Department of the Interior, 1945, 28.
79. Townsend, 129–130.
80. U.S. Department of the Interior, 1945, 28–29.
81. Keegan, 566.
82. Dunnigan and Nofi, 584.
83. Wheal and Pope, 342–343.
84. Dunnigan and Nofi, 68–69.

Chapter 4
85. Keegan, 562–563.
86. Paul, 6–12.
87. Johnson, 54.
88. Paul, 53–54.
89. Paul, 70.
90. William C. Meadows, *Comanche Code Talkers of World War II* (Austin: University of Texas Press, 2002) 66–67.
91. Paul, 82–83, 85–87, 89–91.
92. Ibid., 71, 98.
93. Johnson, 52–61.

Chapter 5
94. Hollis D. Stabler, *No One Ever Asked Me: the World War II Memoirs of an Omaha Indian Soldier,* Victoria Smith, ed. (Lincoln: University of Nebraska Press, 2005), 85, 103.
95. Wheal and Pope, 427–429.
96. Keegan, 350–362.
97. Jones, 126–128.
98. Keegan, 415–433.
99. Jones, 179–187.
100. Kent C. Ware, Sr., personal conversation with author, July 4, 2001.
101. U.S. Department of the Interior, 1945, 50.
102. Ibid., 2.
103. Keegan, 369–386.

104. Jones, 161.
105. Donna J. Matheson, "Warriors Society," Schitsu'umsh: Official Web site of the Coeur d'Alene Tribe, Available online at *http://www.cdatribe-nsn. gov/society.shtml* (accessed December 16, 2006).
106. Bev Pechan, "Legacy of Honor," *Rapid City Journal,* November 9, 2000. Available online at *http://louienet.com/ chiefbaleagle/military.htm.*
107. Wheal and Pope, 101–102.
108. Stabler, 110, 114.
109. Wheal and Pope, 28–29.
110. Meadows, 151–152.
111. Wheal and Pope, 501.
112. Meadows, 155–156.
113. Keegan, 436–446.
114. U.S. Department of the Interior, Bureau of Indian Affairs, *Indian Record, Special Issue: Indians in Military Service* (Washington, D.C.: Government Printing Office, 1970), 5.
115. Bay Pines Native American Council. Available online at *http://www.orgsites.com/fl/ navet* (accessed December 16, 2006).
116. Keegan, 446.
117. Ibid., 510–515.
118. Meadows, 153–154.

Chapter 6
119. Townsend, 33–35.
120. Meadows, 65.
121. Ibid., 92.
122. Ibid., 95.
123. Ibid., 101.
124. Ibid., 141.
125. Ibid., 142–172.
126. Ibid., 206.

Chapter 7

127. Holm, "Fighting a White Man's War," 157–158.
128. Holm, "Fighting a White Man's War," 156.
129. Franco, 99–102.
130. Holm, "Fighting a White Man's War," 156.
131. Franco, 101–105.
132. Ibid. 105–106.
133. Bernstein, 83–85.

Chapter 8

134. Oswald Garrison Villard, "Wardship and the Indian," *Christian Century* 61 (March 29, 1944), 397–398.
135. O. K. Armstrong, "Set the American Indians Free!" *Reader's Digest* (August 1945), 47–49, 52.
136. Donald L. Fixico, *Termination and Relocation: Federal Indian Policy, 1945–1960* (Albuquerque: University of New Mexico Press, 1990), 91–133.
137. Ibid., 134–157.
138. Holm, *Strong Hearts*, 185–187.
139. R. A. Kulka, W. E. Schlenger, J. A. Fairbank, et al., *Trauma and the Vietnam War Generation, Report of the Findings from the National Veterans Readjustment Study* (New York: Bunner/Mazel, 1990).

Bibliography

Abel, Annie Heloise. *The American Indian in the Civil War, 1862–1865.* Lincoln: University of Nebraska Press, 1992.

Alexander, Ted. "Death Song at the Crater: The Chippewa Sharpshooters of Company K." *Civil War: Magazine of the Civil War Society* 10 (September/October 1992): 24–26.

——. "Muskets and Tomahawks." *Civil War: Magazine of the Civil War Society* 10 (September/October 1992): 8–12, 51–52.

Armstrong, O. K. "Set the American Indians Free!" *Reader's Digest* (August 1945): 47–52.

Bay Pines Native American Council. Available online at *http://www.orgsites.com/fl/navet.* Accessed December 16, 2006.

Bellafaire, Judith. "Native American Women Veterans." Women in Military Service for America. Available online at *http://www.womensmemorial.org/Education/NAHM.html.* Accessed December 16, 2006.

Bernstein, Alison R. *American Indians and World War II.* Norman: University of Oklahoma Press, 1991.

Britten, Thomas. *American Indians in World War I.* Albuquerque: University of New Mexico Press, 1997.

Calloway, Colin G. *The American Revolution in Indian Country: Crisis and Diversity in Native American Communities.* New York: Cambridge University Press, 1995.

Cunningham, Frank. *General Stand Watie's Confederate Indians.* Norman: University of Oklahoma Press, 1998.

Dowd, Gregory Evans. *A Spirited Resistance: The North American Indian Struggle for Unity, 1745–1815.* Baltimore: The Johns Hopkins University Press, 1993.

Dunlay, Thomas W. *Wolves for the Blue Soldiers: Indian Scouts and Auxiliaries with the United States Army, 1860–90.* Lincoln: University of Nebraska Press, 1987.

Dunnigan, James F., and Albert A. Nofi. *Victory at Sea: World War II in the Pacific.* New York: William Morrow and Company, 1995.

Enloe, Cynthia H. *Ethnic Soldiers: State Security in Divided Societies.* New York: Penguin Books, 1980.

Fixico, Donald L. *Termination and Relocation: Federal Indian Policy, 1945–1960.* Albuquerque: University of New Mexico Press, 1990.

Foner, Jack D. *The United States Soldier Between Two Wars, 1865–1898.* New York: Humanities Press, 1970.

Franco, Jeré Bishop. *Crossing the Pond: The Native American Effort in World War II.* Denton: University of North Texas Press, 1999.

Garland, Brock. *War Movies.* New York: Facts on File Publications, 1987.

Gearing, Fred. *Priests and Warriors: Social Structures for Cherokee Politics in the 18th Century.* Menasha, Wisc.: American Anthropological Association, 1962.

Grayson, George Washington. *A Creek Warrior for the Confederacy: The Autobiography of Chief G. W. Grayson.* Edited by W. David Baird. Norman: University of Oklahoma Press, 1988.

Hassig, Ross. *Aztec Warfare: Imperial Expansion and Political Control.* Norman: University of Oklahoma Press, 1995.

Hauptman, Lawrence. "War Eagle of the Tuscaroras." *Civil War: Magazine of the Civil War Society* 10 (September/October 1992): 16–17, 27–30.

Holm, Tom. "Fighting a White Man's War: The Extent and Legacy of American Indian Participation in World War II." In *The Plains Indians of the Twentieth Century,* edited by Peter Iverson. Norman: University of Oklahoma Press, 1985: 149–166.

——. *Strong Hearts, Wounded Souls: Native American Veterans of the Vietnam War.* Austin: University of Texas Press, 1996.

——. "American Indian Warfare: The Cycles of Conflict and the Militarization of Native North America." In *A Companion to American Indian History,* edited by Philip J. Deloria and Neal Salisbury. Malden, Mass.: Blackwell Publishers, 2002.

Johnson, Broderick H., ed. *Navajos and World War II.* Tsaile, Ariz.: Navajo Community College Press, 1977.

Jones, James. *WWII: A Chronicle of Soldiering.* New York: Ballantine Books, 1975.

"Joseph J. Clark." 2006. Available online at *www.arlingtoncemetary. net/jjclark.htm.*

Keegan, John. *The Second World War.* New York: Penguin Books, 1990.

Kelly, C. Brian. *Best True Stories from World War II.* New York: Barnes and Noble, 1998.

Kulka, R. A., W. E. Schlenger, J. A. Fairbank, et al. *Trauma and the Vietnam War Generation, Report of the Findings from the National Veterans Readjustment Study.* New York: Bunner/ Mazel, 1990.

Malone, Patrick M. *The Skulking Way of War: Technology and Tactics among the New England Indians.* Baltimore: The Johns Hopkins University Press, 1993.

Matheson, Donna J. "Warriors Society." Schitsu'umsh: Official Web site of the Coeur d'Alene Tribe. Available online at *http://www. cdatribe-nsn.gov/society.shtml.* Accessed December 16, 2006.

Meadows, William C. *Kiowa, Apache, and Comanche Military Societies: Enduring Veterans, 1800 to the Present.* Austin: University of Texas Press, 1999.

——. *Comanche Code Talkers of World War II.* Austin: University of Texas Press, 2002.

Paul, Doris A. *The Navajo Code Talkers.* Philadelphia: Dorrance & Company, 1973.

Pechan, Bev. "Legacy of Honor." *Rapid City Journal,* November 9, 2000. Available online at *http://louienet.com/chiefbaleagle/ military.htm*

Remini, Robert V. *Andrew Jackson and His Indian Wars.* New York: Viking, 2001.

Smith, James. 1799. *An Account of the Remarkable Occurrences in the Life and Travels of Col. James Smith During His Captivity with the Indians in the Years 1755, '56, '57, '58, & '59.* Reprinted in Archibald Loudon. 1808 and 1811. *A Selection of Some of the*

Most Interesting Narratives of Outrages Committed by the Indians in Their Wars with the White People, 2 vols. First reprint Harrisburg: Harrisburg Publishing Company, 1888. Second reprint New York: Arno Press, 1971.

Stabler, Hollis D. *No One Ever Asked Me: the World War II Memoirs of an Omaha Indian Soldier.* Edited by Victoria Smith. Lincoln: University of Nebraska Press, 2005.

Starkey, Armstrong. *European and Native American Warfare, 1675–1815.* Norman: University of Oklahoma Press, 1998.

Sword, Wiley. *President Washington's Indian War: The Struggle for the Old Northwest, 1790–1795.* Norman: University of Oklahoma Press, 1993.

Townsend, Kenneth William. *World War II and the American Indian.* Albuquerque: University of New Mexico Press, 2000.

U.S. Army. "Medal of Honor Citations." Available online at *www.army.mil/cmh-pg/Moh1.htm.* Accessed December 16, 2006.

U.S. Department of the Interior, Bureau of Indian Affairs. *Indian Record, Special Issue: Indians in Military Service.* Washington, D.C.: Government Printing Office, 1970.

U.S. Department of the Interior, Office of Indian Affairs. *Indians in the War.* Chicago: Haskell Printing Department, 1945.

Villard, Oswald Garrison. "Wardship and the Indian." *Christian Century* 61 (March 29, 1944): 397–398.

Ware, Kent C., Sr. "Historical Kiowa Gourd Society." Unpublished manuscript in author's collection. 1996.

Wheal, Elizabeth-Anne, and Stephen Pope. *The Macmillan Dictionary of the Second World War.* London: Macmillan, 1997.

Woodbury, David. "Hasanoanda of the Tonawanda Senecas, an Iroquois at Appomattox Ely S. Parker." *Civil War: Magazine of the Civil War Society* 10 (September/October 1992): 18–23.

———. "From Tahlequah to Boggy Depot: Stand Watie's Civil War." *Civil War: Magazine of the Civil War Society* 10 (September/October 1992): 38–46.

Further Reading

Britten, Thomas. *American Indians in World War I.* Albuquerque: University of New Mexico Press, 1997.

Franco, Jeré Bishop. *Crossing the Pond: The Native American Effort in World War II.* Denton: University of North Texas Press, 1999.

Meadows, William C. *Comanche Code Talkers of World War II.* Austin: University of Texas Press, 2002.

Momaday, N. Scott. *House Made of Dawn.* New York: Perennial Classics, 1999.

Stabler, Hollis. *No One Ever Asked Me: The World War II Memoirs of an Omaha Indian Soldier.* Edited by Victoria Smith. Lincoln: University of Nebraska Press, 2005.

Townsend, Kenneth William. *World War II and the American Indian.* Albuquerque: University of New Mexico Press, 2000.

WEB SITES

Navajo Code Talkers Dictionary
http://www.history.navy.mil/faqs/faq61–4.htm

Navajo Code Talker Association
http://www.lapahie.com/NCTA.cfm

The Navajo Code Talkers Association
http://www.navajocodetalkers.org/

The Comanche Code Talkers of World War II
http://www.utexas.edu/utpress/excerpts/exmeacom.html

Picture Credits

Index